If Your Adolescent Has ADHD

THE ANNENBERG
PUBLIC POLICY CENTER
OF THE UNIVERSITY OF PENNSYLVANIA

Daniel Romer, PhD, Director of Research

The Annenberg Foundation Trust at
SUNNYLANDS

The Adolescent Mental Health Initiative of the Annenberg
Public Policy Center and the Sunnylands Trust

Patrick E. Jamieson, PhD, *series editor*

Other books in the series

*If Your Adolescent Has Depression
or Bipolar Disorder*
Dwight L. Evans, MD, and Linda Wasmer Andrews

If Your Adolescent Has an Eating Disorder
B. Timothy Walsh, MD, and V.L. Cameron

If Your Adolescent Has Schizophrenia
Raquel E. Gur, MD, PhD, and Ann Braden Johnson, PhD

If Your Adolescent Has an Anxiety Disorder
Edna B. Foa, PhD, and Linda Wasmer Andrews

If Your Adolescent Has ADHD

An Essential Resource for Parents

Thomas J. Power, PhD
Linda Wasmer Andrews

THE ANNENBERG
PUBLIC POLICY CENTER
OF THE UNIVERSITY OF PENNSYLVANIA

The Adolescent Mental Health Initiative of the Annenberg
Public Policy Center and the Sunnylands Trust

The Annenberg Foundation Trust at
SUNNYLANDS

OXFORD
UNIVERSITY PRESS

OXFORD
UNIVERSITY PRESS

Oxford University Press is a department of the University of Oxford. It furthers
the University's objective of excellence in research, scholarship, and education
by publishing worldwide. Oxford is a registered trade mark of Oxford University
Press in the UK and certain other countries.

Published in the United States of America by Oxford University Press
198 Madison Avenue, New York, NY 10016, United States of America.

© Oxford University Press 2018

Library of Congress Cataloging-in-Publication Data
Names: Power, Thomas J., author. | Andrews, Linda Wasmer, author.
Title: If your adolescent has ADHD : an essential resource for parents /
Thomas J. Power, PhD, and Linda Wasmer Andrews.
Description: New York, NY : Oxford University Press, [2018] |
Series: The adolescent mental health initiative of the Annenberg Public Policy Center
and the Sunnylands Trust
Identifiers: LCCN 2017037994 | ISBN 9780190494636 (pbk. : alk. paper) |
ISBN 9780190873103 (hardcover : alk. paper)
Subjects: LCSH: Attention-deficit hyperactivity disorder in adolescence. |
Attention-deficit disordered youth. | Parents of attention-deficit disordered children.
Classification: LCC RJ506.H9 P69 2018 |
DDC 616.85/8900835—dc23
LC record available at https://lccn.loc.gov/2017037994

9 8 7 6 5 4 3 2

Paperback printed by Sheridan Books, Inc., United States of America
Hardback printed by Bridgeport National Bindery, Inc., United States of America

Disclosure

This project was not supported by any external direct or indirect funding. The Children's Hospital of Philadelphia has received funding from Pfizer and Shire to support Dr. Power's involvement in physician and parent educational activities. The views expressed in this book are those of the authors and may not represent the positions of Pfizer and Shire. The use of brand names in this publication does not imply endorsement by the authors or imply criticism of similar products not mentioned.

Contents

Three

Finding the Best Treatment for Your Teen:
Behavioral Approaches   42

Four

Finding the Best Treatment for Your Teen:
ADHD Medications   69

Five

Your Teen at Home: Building Strong Bonds and Positive
Behavior Patterns   102

Six

Your Teen in the Community: Fostering Friendships and Safe Choices   131

Seven

Your Teen at School: Promoting Smart Learning and Study Strategies   157

Eight

Transition to Adulthood: Supporting Independence, Staying Involved   183

Acknowledgments

Dr. Power would like to thank Nathan Blum, MD, and Patty Huang, MD, of The Children's Hospital of Philadelphia, who generously shared their insights and expertise on ADHD medications.

Ms. Andrews would like to thank the parents she interviewed for this book, who kindly shared their families' stories so that others can learn from their experience and benefit from their encouragement.

If Your Adolescent Has ADHD

Chapter One

Introduction: Same Old ADHD, Brand-New Teenage Challenges

One major milestone of adolescence is getting a first driver's license—and one milestone of parenting an adolescent is handing over the keys to the family car for the first time. Imagine yourself standing by the street outside your home, waving as your teen pulls away from the curb for an inaugural spin around the neighborhood. Chances are, you'll be counting every second until your teen returns. For a 15-minute drive, that's 900 nerve-racking seconds, each one fraught with a complicated mix of fear and pride.

When your child has ADHD, your parental anxiety may be ratcheted up several notches. ADHD—short for attention-deficit/hyperactivity disorder—is a condition characterized by persistent problems with paying attention, controlling impulsive behavior, or being overactive. In adolescents, inattention and impulsivity tend to be especially pronounced, and those aren't helpful traits behind the wheel of a car.

The truth is, inexperienced teen drivers in general are far more likely than adults to get into motor vehicle accidents, and ADHD just heightens the risk. Research shows that teens with ADHD are more likely to be cited for reckless driving and to have accidents resulting in injury or death than teens without the condition. Yet there's another important truth to keep in mind: Most people with ADHD learn how to control their attention and impulses behind the wheel and go on to become safe, responsible drivers.

Of course, learning to drive is just one of a host of challenges facing adolescents as they navigate the tricky terrain between childhood and adulthood. This is a period during which young people are adjusting, academically and socially, to middle school, high school, and college. They're forging independent identities and forming new attachments. Meanwhile, they're often making high-stakes choices about alcohol, drugs, and sexual activity.

Having ADHD multiplies the challenges in all these situations. Teens with ADHD are more likely to engage in risky sexual behavior, drink alcohol, smoke, and abuse drugs, compared to their peers without the condition. At the same time, they're at high risk for school-related problems, such as leaving classwork or homework incomplete, getting low grades, scoring poorly on standardized tests, and eventually dropping out of school.

In this book, we take a clear-eyed look at the risks and challenges that go along with having ADHD. We don't gloss over reality, but we do describe workable ways of creating a more positive reality for your child. Today, we know more than ever before about how to help adolescents manage their ADHD. We'll tell you about the most up-to-date, scientifically grounded approaches. There's solid evidence that these approaches can help teens with ADHD thrive at home, flourish at school, and succeed in the community.

Five Key Skills for Parents

Raising *any* adolescent is complicated. But when your child has ADHD, the complexity is increased exponentially. In these pages, you'll find facts, strategies, and tips that help make your job a little less daunting and more manageable.

We'll discuss the hands-on specifics of successful parenting strategies, classroom approaches, behavioral therapy, and drug treatment. We'll describe effective ways to communicate with your teen, encourage good study habits, and foster healthy friendships. Unlike many ADHD books, which are often aimed at parents of younger children, we'll also talk about issues unique to the teen years, such as how to help your child stay safe behind the wheel, make smart choices away from home, succeed at a summer job, and get ready for college.

As you read, you may notice that certain themes keep cropping up time and again. In fact, much of the information in this book can be boiled down to five key parenting skills:

- Preparing yourself to face new challenges as your child with ADHD gets older
- Informing yourself about the best tools and techniques for managing teen ADHD
- Maintaining a strong attachment with your child throughout the adolescent years
- Supporting your child's budding independence while staying involved in his or her life
- Building partnerships with the other adults in your child's life, including therapists, doctors, teachers, and coaches

Like other skills, these can be improved with practice. We offer ample suggestions for how to put these skills into action at home and when to reach out for professional support.

This book is a guide to what works for managing adolescent ADHD—and what doesn't—based on the latest research. Some of the approaches discussed here, such as school-based mentoring and youth involvement in sports and extracurricular activities, show great promise but have received relatively little attention elsewhere.

The Faces Behind the Pages

This book was created under the auspices of the Annenberg Public Policy Center (APPC) of the University of Pennsylvania, one of the premier communication policy centers in the United States. In the early 2000s, APPC launched an initiative aimed at spreading the word about adolescent mental health issues. It convened a panel of experts and published a series of books on several mental and behavioral health conditions affecting teens, including depression, bipolar disorder, anxiety disorders, substance abuse, eating disorders, schizophrenia, and suicide.

Something was missing, however: None of the original books addressed ADHD—a common condition, but one that has only recently begun to garner the attention it deserves in adolescents. Recognizing an unmet need, APPC decided it was time to add a new title to the series. You're reading the book that resulted.

Dr. Power, the lead author of this book, is director of the Center for Management of ADHD at Children's Hospital of Philadelphia. This multidisciplinary center serves youth between the ages of 3 and 18. Dr. Power is also professor of school psychology in pediatrics, psychiatry, and education at the University of Pennsylvania. He has conducted extensive research in children and adolescents who have ADHD, and he has a particular interest in developing interventions that promote family and school success.

The second author of this book is a journalist who has specialized in writing about mental health issues for more than three decades. She co-authored six of the original books in the APPC series. One of her most important contributions to the current book was to interview parents of adolescents with ADHD from across the United States. These moms and dads generously shared their experiences because they know first-hand how valuable parent-to-parent support can be.

Many parents spoke candidly in their interviews about intimate matters, including family conflicts and personal feelings. To protect their privacy, the names of parents, teens, and other family members mentioned in this book have been changed. But although the names are fictitious, the stories are true and filled with the hard-earned wisdom of lived experience. We think you'll find the insights and encouragement shared by these parents especially powerful.

How to Use This Book

We would love for you to read this book from cover to cover. However, we know that isn't always practical, so we've designed the book so that each chapter can stand alone. Within each chapter, you'll see several subheadings, which serve as signposts pointing you toward the exact information you're seeking. Here's a quick glance at what the various chapters contain:

- Chapter Two. Essential Facts. This chapter provides the basic background information you need in order to understand what ADHD is and how it may be affecting your teen. Even if you plan to skip ahead in the book, we recommend reading this chapter first to get a good grounding in the issues. Inside this chapter, you'll find information about ADHD symptoms, diagnosis, prevalence rates, and risk factors. You'll learn about other conditions that often occur alongside ADHD. Plus, you'll read about experiences and behaviors that help your teen meet the challenges of ADHD successfully.

- Chapter Three. Behavioral Approaches. This chapter introduces the behavioral principles and approaches that play a major role in managing ADHD. Within this chapter, you'll learn about the ABCs (antecedents, behavior, and consequences) of behavior change. You'll also find plain-language explanations of key behavioral therapy concepts, such as positive reinforcement, negative reinforcement, strategic punishment, and planned ignoring. Other topics include finding a therapist, paying for therapy, and participating in parent training, family therapy, and home-based behavioral strategies.

- Chapter Four. ADHD Medications. Most teens with ADHD benefit from taking medication in addition to using behavioral approaches to manage their condition. This chapter explores the pros and cons of drug treatment. It covers both stimulant and non-stimulant medications that have been approved for treating ADHD. You'll find tips on encouraging teens to take their medication as prescribed. In addition, you'll read about educating teens on the dangers of misusing, selling, or giving away their medication.

- Chapter Five. Your Teen at Home. ADHD can put a strain on family relationships and compound the challenges of raising a teenager. This chapter discusses proven parenting strategies that can help bridge a communication gap, mend a damaged relationship, and encourage more positive interactions at home. It builds on the behavioral concepts discussed in Chapter Three, so we recommend reading that chapter first. In this chapter, you'll learn about the effective use of rewards, strategic punishment, and behavioral contracts. Other topics include setting and enforcing curfews, promoting healthy sleep habits, and staying involved in your teen's life without being overly intrusive.

- Chapter Six. Your Teen in the Community. Teens with ADHD often have difficulty making and keeping friends. Many are neglected, rejected, or bullied by their peers. This chapter discusses how to help your teen form healthy friendships and resist negative peer pressure. It also looks at the benefits of extracurricular activities, and it offers tips on encouraging your teen to participate. Toward the end of the chapter, you'll learn more about the risks faced by teen drivers with ADHD. You'll find step-by-step guidelines on things you can do to reduce those risks and foster safe driving habits.

- Chapter Seven. Your Teen at School. This chapter is devoted to strategies for overcoming the academic hurdles faced by middle school and high school students with ADHD. It discusses how to identify effective teachers and support positive student–teacher relationships. It explains how school personnel may create a formal, written educational plan for your teen when needed, and it looks at your role in this process. Plus, it describes common classroom accommodations and promising school-based interventions, such as mentoring programs. In the chapter's closing pages, you'll find a step-by-step plan for helping teens manage their homework and study time more efficiently.

- Chapter Eight. Transition to Adulthood. At least half of kids diagnosed with ADHD still meet the full criteria for the condition as young adults, and many others have some lingering symptoms. This chapter explores how ADHD may continue affecting your child when going to college, starting a career, or moving away from home. In the realm of higher education, it offers questions to ask when choosing a college, and it explains how to request classroom accommodations when needed. In the world of work, it describes the characteristics of an ADHD-friendly work environment, and it provides examples of simple adjustments that may enhance job performance and productivity.

Tips on Finding What You Need Quickly

We've tried to make it as easy as possible to find the information you're seeking, whether it's located within this book or in an outside resource. These tips may help:

- If you want to delve deeper into a specific subject, let us point the way. At numerous places throughout this book, we mention websites that provide further details on a particular issue. At the end of every chapter, we also highlight at least one online resource where you can learn more.
- If you want to read more about ADHD in general, turn to the appendix, Resources for Parents and Teens, at the back of this book. It lists organizations, websites, and other books that provide helpful information about ADHD and related conditions.

- If you're a health or mental health professional or an educator, check out the appendix, Books for ADHD Professionals.

- If you don't remember what a scientific or educational term means, flip to the Glossary at the back of this book.

- If you're interested in non-standard ADHD treatments, keep reading! We've focused primarily on behavioral approaches and medication in these pages because they're considered the gold-standard treatments for ADHD. There's strong scientific evidence to support their effectiveness. However, we know that you may be curious about other approaches as well, so we've discussed them more briefly at relevant places throughout the book. Among the topics addressed are complementary approaches in general (Chapter Three), neurofeedback (Chapter Three), executive function training (Chapter Three), meditation and yoga (Chapter Three), fatty acid supplements (Chapter Four), elimination diets (Chapter Five), and physical exercise (Chapter Six).

At the end of every chapter, you'll find a short list of Key Points. These are some of the most significant take-home messages from that chapter. If there's one overriding message we hope you take away from the book as a whole, it's this: Parenting an adolescent with ADHD feels less overwhelming once you learn some essential skills and strategies and know where to find further guidance and support.

Chapter Two

ADHD from A to Z: Essential Facts You Need to Know

Early on, you probably noticed that your child had a lot more trouble than other kids with resisting distractions, staying organized, sitting still, or thinking things through before acting. Perhaps you were looking forward to the day when your child would outgrow these tendencies. If so, adolescence may have brought a big surprise: The reality is, most children with ADHD grow into preteens and teens with ADHD.

Often, that realization comes as a wake-up call. By late elementary school, you might have felt as if you were finally getting a handle on how to raise a distractible, hyperactive, or impulsive child. Then middle school and high school arrived, bringing a whole new set of challenges. The schoolwork is much harder now. And the expectations for your child— such as driving, babysitting, holding down a summer job, and filling out college applications—are much bigger and more consequential.

Meanwhile, your child's behavior may be in flux. Instead of cutting up in class and talking nonstop at home, your child may suddenly be failing tests, acting defiant, or hanging out with the wrong crowd. The parenting strategies that worked so well just a few short years ago may have gone out the window. Many parents are left feeling confused, frustrated, and doubting their own child-rearing ability.

If you're feeling that way, here are three things to remember, which underlie everything else you'll read in this book:

- ADHD is a real, brain-based condition, not an indictment of your parenting ability or your child's character.
- Changes in behavior are very common in adolescents in general—and changes in behavioral symptoms are very common in adolescents with ADHD.
- You can learn strategies and find resources that help you and your child manage the teenage version of ADHD.

Snapshots of Teen ADHD

No two teens and their parents have exactly the same experiences. But chances are, you can relate to the ups and downs, large and small, of other parents raising adolescents with ADHD. Following are a couple of stories shared by parents who volunteered to be interviewed for this book. You'll find other family stories sprinkled throughout these pages.

Emily's Story

Emily is no longer the little ball of perpetual motion that she was in first grade, when her ADHD was diagnosed. But at age 16, she still finds it difficult to sit still or stand in one place for long.

"If we're in a restaurant and she's finished her dinner, she'll ask everyone sitting there at the table if she can stand," says her mother, Melissa. "It takes people a little aback if they aren't used to her, but most don't seem to mind. If we go to a movie theater, she'll sit on the aisle seat so she has more room for her body to move around."

Her close-knit group of friends, who have known each other for years, take it in stride. "She'll say, 'I'm hyper, hyper,' and they'll laugh," says Melissa. "Sometimes they'll ask, 'Did you take your pill?' I think Emily relies a lot on her old friends because they're safe. She's just the quirky one, and they all understand her."

Other kids aren't always so accepting. "She's got this impulsive thing where, out of nowhere, she'll jab someone or throw a pencil," Melissa says. Not surprisingly, this behavior has caused some annoyance among the other students. Emily is making an effort to improve her impulse control, but it's still a work in progress.

In the meantime, Emily has to deal with taunts from some of her classmates about what they see as her childish behavior. "There's this stigma attached to ADHD," says Melissa. "People want to know why she can't just get control of herself, and she's always hearing that she's too willful. It makes her very insecure and very anxious. I mean, she struggles with that *a lot*. Kids are so vulnerable in high school."

Jayden's Story

Jayden doesn't have a problem keeping his body still. For him, the challenge is getting his mind to settle on one thing for more than a couple of minutes. At school, the 13-year-old finds it especially difficult to focus on writing and math. "His grades aren't terrible, because somehow he manages to do well on tests," says his mother, Angela. Yet he's always falling behind, because he has trouble paying attention in class, following directions, and remembering homework.

When Jayden was younger, ADHD medication helped him manage these issues. "While he was on his medication, he could actually do writing assignments," Angela says. "But he didn't like taking it, because he said it made him feel out of it. My husband and I weren't completely comfortable with the medication, either."

So last year, when Jayden was in seventh grade, he and his parents decided to stop the medication. Now they're rethinking that decision, however, because eighth grade has turned into an ordeal. "Off his medication, getting any work done is very, very difficult for him," Angela says.

Lately, Jayden's frustration with school has begun boiling over at home. "A lot of stuff has started coming out—a lot of anger," says Angela. "His tolerance is so low, he gets annoyed at almost anything his younger brother does. His brother coughs, and it bothers him, and that leads to yelling and fighting. Some days, it seems like we need to hide from the kid."

When Angela is feeling exasperated, she often turns to a network of online friends for support. "I belong to four Facebook groups for parents of kids with ADHD," she says. "Sometimes, I might get an idea from another parent about how to handle a particular problem. Mostly, though, it just makes me feel better to know I'm not the only one dealing with this stuff."

ADHD or Just Being a Teenager?

Emily's and Jayden's experiences of ADHD are quite different, and your child's unique story undoubtedly has its own twists and turns. ADHD is a complex condition that can cause a wide variety of symptoms. These symptoms can be grouped into three categories: inattentive, hyperactive/impulsive, and combined.

In the past, these categories were called "subtypes." That term seemed to imply a relatively stable classification, like having type 1 or type 2 diabetes. However, ADHD often presents itself differently at different points in the lifespan. For example, a young person with ADHD might have mainly symptoms of hyperactivity as a preschooler, symptoms of hyperactivity and inattention as an older child, and mainly symptoms of inattention as a teen. In recognition of this fact, ADHD categories are now known as "presentations," referring to how the condition presents at a particular time in a person's life.

As you read through the descriptions of ADHD presentations in the next sections, you'll notice that many of the listed behaviors sound quite common. Rare is the teen who has never misplaced a phone, put off writing a report, or neglected to take out the trash. To meet the criteria for ADHD, these behaviors must be part of a broader, dysfunctional pattern that is outside the norm for the teen's developmental level. This behavioral pattern leads to problems in two or more settings, such as in school, at home, in after-school activities, with friends, or at a job.

To be considered a disorder, ADHD symptoms must seriously interfere with a teen's daily life or development. These are some facets of teen life that are often affected:

- Getting along with family members
- Making and keeping friends
- Performing academically in school
- Finishing and turning in homework
- Controlling behavior at school
- Having positive self-esteem

Inattentive Presentation

Inattention refers to difficulty staying mentally focused. The kinds of behaviors that are typical of adolescents with the inattentive form of ADHD include the following:

- Not paying close attention to detail, even when they like what they're doing
- Making "silly" mistakes on tests, even when they know the answers
- Having trouble paying attention to anything for an extended period
- Finding it hard to stay focused long enough to read a book chapter
- Not listening to what others say, even when spoken to directly
- Seeming as if they are always distracted during conversation
- Starting to do their homework, but quickly becoming sidetracked
- Having a backpack so messy that they can never find what they need
- Missing homework due dates or getting to class late frequently
- Putting off writing reports or filling out college applications until too late
- Losing their eyeglasses, school supplies, wallet, keys, or phone repeatedly
- Finding it hard to tune out irrelevant sights and sounds when studying
- Neglecting to do chores or run errands that they intended to do
- Forgetting to keep appointments or meet up with friends as planned

Hyperactive/Impulsive Presentation

Hyperactivity refers to excessive physical movement or to extreme talkativeness or restlessness. *Impulsivity* refers to hasty actions made without giving any thought to the possible repercussions. The kinds of behaviors that are typical of adolescents with the hyperactive/impulsive form of ADHD include the following:

- Squirming or fidgeting when they're expected to sit still
- Having a habit of repeatedly bouncing a leg or tapping a foot
- Walking around the classroom at inappropriate times
- Being unable to enjoy any quiet hobbies or leisure pastimes
- Finding it difficult to sit through a movie or restaurant meal
- Feeling restless, jittery, or impatient much of the time
- Being always on the go, to a degree that others find exhausting
- Chattering constantly, to the point where others become annoyed
- Blurting out rude or thoughtless comments without thinking
- Yelling out an answer without waiting for the question to be finished
- Not waiting for their turn in conversation or during games
- Finding it exceptionally difficult to wait in checkout lines
- Butting into other people's private conversations
- Barging into other people's activities without being invited

Combined Presentation

It's common for teens whose behavior falls mainly into the inattentive category to also have some hyperactive/impulsive symptoms, and vice versa. Some teens have enough symptoms of each ADHD presentation to meet the diagnostic criteria for both inattentive and hyperactive/impulsive ADHD. This is known as the combined presentation.

From Hyper Child to Disorganized Teen

Before you were the parent of an adolescent with ADHD, you were the parent of a young child with the same behavioral tendencies. Even if your child's ADHD wasn't formally diagnosed until later, you probably had inklings of it from an early age.

After years of practice, you might have expected your family to have a handle on ADHD by now. If that's not the case, you may wonder where your family went wrong. When you're feeling this way, it's time for a reality check: Even if you, your teen, and the rest of your family have done an outstanding job of coping with ADHD thus far, you may still need to make some adjustments at this point in your child's life.

That's because ADHD is a moving target. The symptoms that are causing your child the most trouble today may be different from those that caused the biggest problems a decade ago.

Changes in Presentation

Some parents say they first noticed that a child with ADHD was extra-active as far back as the toddler years. It can be hard to distinguish ADHD from normal differences in activity level in children that young. By elementary school, however, it's usually clear that something out of the ordinary is going on.

Hyperactivity is often prominent in younger children with ADHD. The most obvious signs of hyperactivity, such as running around a classroom, tend to peak at five to six years old. After that, they gradually decline. By adolescence, hyperactivity tends to decrease or become less noticeable. When it's still present, the symptoms usually take a subtler form, such as fidgeting or feeling restless.

Impulsivity often diminishes in adolescence as well, but it may still cause significant problems. For example, poor impulse control may lead to social blunders, such as blurting out thoughtless remarks or butting into private conversations. Such missteps interfere with making friends and increase the risk of teasing and rejection.

By comparison, inattention declines less rapidly as children get older. During the teen years, problems caused by inattention may come to the fore as academic demands increase and expectations of personal independence grow. As you read through this book, you'll notice that many coping strategies for adolescents with ADHD aim to help them harness their attention, manage their time, and organize their activities.

Rising Rates and Diagnostic Debates

ADHD is certainly more discussed today than it was when you were young. There's growing awareness that some behaviors that might once have been labeled "bad" or "lazy" are actually symptomatic of a brain-based condition. But is ADHD actually much more prevalent than it once was? The answer to that question requires a bit of explanation.

A few years back, researchers from the Centers for Disease Control and Prevention (CDC) released some alarming statistics that garnered a lot of media attention: In 2011, 11% of U.S. children and teens (ages 4 to 17) were reported to have been diagnosed with ADHD, based on a large, national survey of parents. That's up from 7.8% in 2003 and 9.5% in 2007—a whopping 42% increase in a mere eight years.

To interpret these startling-sounding statistics, however, you need to consider how the CDC data were collected. These prevalence figures came from parent reports of diagnoses made by family health care providers. The CDC researchers didn't independently confirm that the diagnoses were accurate, so it's quite possible that some mistakes were made.

In an ideal world, all health care providers would conduct a comprehensive, best-practices evaluation before diagnosing ADHD. Unfortunately, in the real world, that doesn't always happen. Some children and teens who are inattentive or very active—but whose symptoms don't actually rise to the level of ADHD or who aren't seriously impaired in their daily lives—end up being inaccurately diagnosed.

It's also conceivable that some parents may have jumped to the wrong conclusion. For example, a doctor might have recommended that a child be further evaluated for ADHD, but the parent might have heard this as a definite diagnosis rather than a possibility to be investigated. Still, it seems doubtful that parental confusion could be the only explanation.

Such a sharp increase in reported prevalence rates raises legitimate concerns about overdiagnosis of ADHD, which may lead to overprescribing of ADHD medication. This is a particular concern in affluent, suburban communities. In rural areas, in some inner-city neighborhoods, and with some ethnic minority groups, ADHD may still be *under*diagnosed and *under*treated.

How prevalent is ADHD when best-practice evaluation methods are applied? Although there's some dispute about the true answer to that question, the emerging consensus is that about 7% of youth actually meet the diagnostic criteria for ADHD. That's a sizable percentage, to be sure. But it's significantly less than the 11% reported in the CDC survey.

The ADHD Gender Gap

Among youth ages 12 to 17, boys are more likely than girls to have been diagnosed with ADHD. To some extent, this may reflect a real difference between the sexes. But it may also partly reflect a bias toward thinking of ADHD as a guy thing.

Girls with ADHD are more likely to have mainly symptoms of inattention. Such symptoms are easier for parents, teachers, and family doctors to overlook than hyperactivity. As a result, girls are referred less often for evaluation and treatment. Yet ADHD doesn't have to be loud and rowdy to cause trouble. The inattentive form of ADHD is associated with significant problems at school, at home, and in relationships.

Years ago, it was thought that boys were four to six times more likely to have ADHD than girls. More recent research suggests that boys are actually only about two to two-and-a-half times more likely to have the condition.

Getting an Accurate Diagnosis

Even for a trained professional, it's not easy to tell at a glance whether an adolescent has full-blown ADHD. After all, virtually every teen gets distracted, acts impulsively, or seems restless now and then. Sorting out the nature and extent of a teen's symptoms and ruling out other possible causes takes time and expertise. Yet health care professionals are often under pressure to make a rapid diagnosis, and that can lead to mistakes.

If your child's diagnosis has not yet been firmly established, start by making an appointment with your child's doctor. The doctor can check for other possible causes of ADHD-like symptoms, such as hearing problems, sleep disorders, or undetected seizures that can mimic inattention. Many primary care doctors are also skilled at conducting a preliminary assessment for ADHD. However, most are less familiar with ADHD in adolescents than in younger children. Also, primary care doctors usually are not specialists in assessing the other emotional, behavioral, and learning problems that often go along with ADHD.

When your child's doctor suspects ADHD, your next step should generally be to seek an in-depth evaluation by a qualified mental health professional, such as a child and adolescent psychiatrist or clinical psychologist. The professional can assess your child's emotional, social, and academic functioning. Plus, the professional can evaluate other factors that might be affecting your child instead of or in addition to ADHD. Here's a quick overview of some of the assessment procedures that may be used.

Clinical Interviews

In a clinical interview, the mental health professional talks with your child about symptoms, concerns, and relationships at home, at school, and in the community. Be ready for the professional to also ask *you* questions about your child's

- Development and health history
- Past behavior
- Current lifestyle
- Ongoing symptoms
- Possible co-occurring problems
- Parent–teen relationships
- Sibling interactions

In addition, whenever possible, it's helpful if the mental health professional can interview some of your child's teachers to get their points of view. Other adults in your child's life may see behavior that's different from how your child behaves around you. Plus, teachers may provide insight into the social and educational climate of the school.

Rating Scales

Rating scales are a quick, easy way to evaluate your child's behavior. They provide valuable information about how your child's behavior compares to that of other adolescents of the same age and sex. Rating scales for assessing ADHD are ideally completed by both parents and teachers—and it's helpful to have input from multiple teachers, if possible.

The mental health professional may also ask your child to complete rating scales. Teens with ADHD often underestimate the seriousness of their difficulties. It's helpful for the professional to know the extent to which your teen's self-rating is similar to that of adults who know your child well.

Many ratings scales have been developed to assess ADHD symptoms and coexisting problems. Typically, the mental health professional will use a scale that is specifically designed to assess ADHD symptoms and impairments as well as a scale that assesses a broader range of emotional and behavioral concerns.

Differential Diagnosis

Just as the doctor needed to rule out alternate medical explanations for your child's symptoms, the mental health professional needs to rule out other mental, emotional, and behavioral conditions that can resemble ADHD. Many of the interview questions you answer and the rating scales you fill out will be geared to this purpose. Examples of conditions that may be confused with ADHD include anxiety, depression, learning disorders, conduct problems, and substance abuse.

Comorbidity Assessment

In some cases, the mental health professional may discover that your teen meets the diagnostic criteria for both ADHD and another condition. *Comorbidity* is the technical term for the coexistence of two or more health conditions in the same individual. If your child has a comorbid condition, it needs to be thoroughly evaluated as well. The mental health professional may do this assessment or refer your child to another health care provider for further evaluation.

What About Neuropsych Testing?

Neuropsychological testing uses standardized tasks to evaluate psychological processes that are related to particular brain structures and functions. Examples include computerized tests of executive functioning—the brain processes involved in organizing information, planning future actions, and regulating behavior and emotions. Such brain processes include the ability to shift attention when required and the ability to hold back the first reaction to a stimulus and respond in a more considered way.

This type of testing usually isn't part of the standard assessment for ADHD. However, it may be useful when there's evidence of a brain injury or a medical illness affecting the brain, such as a brain tumor. In such cases, neuropsychological testing may help the health professional identify which brain processes are affected, plan treatment strategies, and monitor the teen's progress.

The Comorbidity Double Whammy

Previously in this chapter, you met Emily. In addition to having ADHD, she has been diagnosed with an anxiety disorder. "Her anxiety really spiked in eighth grade," recalls her mother. "Then it died down for a while, but it resurged in ninth grade when my mom passed away. By the end of ninth grade,

Emily's teachers were increasing their demands, and Emily had so much anxiety about her schoolwork that it was difficult for her to even go to school."

Worries about teasing by classmates only made Emily's anxiety worse. At times, she would have panic attacks—abrupt waves of intense fear and apprehension accompanied by physical symptoms, such as stomach pains, nausea, and dizziness.

In response, Emily's mother began taking her to see a therapist. The therapist taught Emily calming techniques, such as breathing exercises, which she now uses at the first sign of rising anxiety. This year, in 10th grade, Emily is having fewer panic attacks. Yet gaining the upper hand on ADHD and anxiety remains a work in progress.

Emily's experience is far from unique. In fact, when it comes to ADHD, comorbidity is the rule rather than the exception. The majority of adolescents with ADHD have at least one other emotional, behavioral, or learning disorder. Such disorders interact with ADHD, often worsening the symptoms and making it harder to succeed in daily life. To reduce the added distress and disruption, it's crucial to identify and treat any comorbid conditions.

Discussed next are some conditions that often occur side by side with ADHD. To learn more about them, check Resources for Parents and Teens at the end of this book.

Anxiety Disorders

Believe it or not, anxiety can be a good thing. A little anxiety before a big test helps boost alertness, and reasonable apprehension about getting into the car with a drunk driver helps your child stay safe. This type of healthy anxiety is appropriate to the situation, and it goes away soon after the threatening situation has passed.

By contrast, anxiety disorders lead to fear or worry that is excessive, persistent, and difficult to control. Teens may begin going to great lengths to avoid things that trigger their anxiety. Some, like Emily, experience full-on panic attacks. To rise to the level of a disorder, anxiety must be severe enough to cause significant problems in daily life. Without treatment, these problems may get worse over time.

About one-fourth of children and teens with ADHD have an anxiety disorder. The two conditions often feed each other. ADHD can interfere with a teen's ability to succeed in school and connect with peers, which may lead to stress, worry, and self-consciousness. An anxiety disorder may magnify those feelings to the point where they're disabling. To help the teen feel more at ease and confident, treatment needs to address both ADHD and anxiety.

Depression

In casual conversation, people may refer to themselves as depressed any time they feel a bit down in the dumps. In the mental health world, however, the term *depression* has a more specific meaning. Teens who meet the formal criteria for major depression feel down, empty, hopeless, or irritable for weeks on end. They may lose interest in most things they once enjoyed, and they may pull away from family and friends.

Major depression can cause a wide range of other troublesome symptoms as well, such as changes in eating and sleeping habits, frequent tiredness, feelings of worthlessness, and, at times, thoughts of suicide. In some individuals, depression leads to restless overactivity and reduced ability to concentrate—symptoms that bear a striking resemblance to the hyperactivity and inattention of ADHD. A thorough, professional evaluation is needed to determine whether a teen with these symptoms has ADHD, depression, or both.

When ADHD and depression occur together, they often make each other worse. ADHD may lead to repeated negative interactions with parents, teachers, and peers. These experiences are demoralizing, and they only add to depressed feelings of hopelessness, helplessness, and low self-esteem. Depression, in turn, may sap a teen's motivation, making it harder to marshal the effort needed to get ADHD symptoms under control. When a teen is stuck in this negative cycle, treatment needs to address both ADHD and depression.

Disruptive Mood Dysregulation Disorder

Depressive feelings may also manifest as disruptive mood dysregulation disorder (DMDD)—a relatively new diagnosis in the mental health field. The hallmark of this disorder is persistent irritability and frequent, severe temper outbursts. Teens with DMDD tend to lash out when feeling frustrated—for example, by yelling, throwing things, or hitting someone. Even when they aren't flying into a rage, teens with DMDD are in a chronically cranky or angry mood.

The constant irritability and hair-trigger temper of DMDD go far beyond normal teenage moodiness. DMDD can wreak havoc with relationships. Also, because teens with DMDD have a low tolerance for frustration, they tend to give up quickly on challenging tasks, which may limit their success in school, sports, and other activities.

Only a small fraction of teens with ADHD meet the full diagnostic criteria for DMDD. However, many more youth with ADHD have milder problems with handling frustration and managing difficult emotions. Some have rapid mood swings, and they may be unaware of exactly what is triggering these sudden changes in mood. Teens with such symptoms may benefit from treatment approaches that help them with emotion control and communication skills.

Oppositional Defiant Disorder and Conduct Disorder

Other conditions can also cause a lot of upheaval in the lives of teens and their families. Oppositional defiant disorder (ODD) is characterized by an ongoing pattern of frequent defiance, hostility, and spitefulness. Some pushback against authority is a natural, and often healthy, part of growing up. In teens with ODD, however, stubbornly refusing to cooperate with adults and arguing with authority figures can become a constant source of tension.

ODD is one of the most frequent of all comorbidities in teens with ADHD. In many cases, the roots may lie in deep-seated frustration, which builds up after years of repeatedly experiencing failure or getting into trouble for behavior they can't control. In addition, many teens with ADHD have a neurobiological disposition to be moody, irritable, and temperamental. This may manifest in defiant, oppositional behavior.

Conduct disorder is another very disruptive condition. It's characterized by frequent behaviors that violate important social norms or the basic rights of others. Some teens with conduct disorder engage in aggressive behavior, such as bullying, carrying weapons, or getting into physical fights. Others destroy property, lie, steal, skip school, or stay out past curfew. This is more than just ordinary teenage rebelliousness. It's a persistent pattern of behavior that gets teens into serious trouble at home, at school, and sometimes with police.

Teens with conduct disorder can be split into two groups depending on when the first signs of the disorder appeared: early onset (before age 10) or later onset (age 10 or later). Early-onset conduct disorder is considered more serious. However, both early-onset and later-onset conduct disorder can put teens at high risk for substance abuse, delinquent behavior, and involvement with the juvenile justice system.

Teens with ADHD often fail to do what parents or teachers ask because they aren't paying attention or become distracted. Teens with ODD or conduct disorder often choose to defy adult requests or break the rules. When both types of behavior are combined, teens face a double dose of trouble. They may quickly earn a reputation for being particularly uncooperative or unruly. To help keep problems from escalating and steer behavior in a most positive direction, treatment should address ODD or conduct disorder as well as ADHD.

Learning Disorders

Learning disorders affect teens' ability to perform up to their potential in school and to use reading, writing, or math skills in everyday life. These disorders are identified by the specific skills that are affected. For example, dyslexia impairs the ability to read and spell, and dyscalculia impairs the ability to understand and use numerical information. Teens with learning disorders read, write, or do math at a level lower than what would be expected based on their age, grade level, or developmental level.

For many students with learning disorders, school is an uphill battle from day one. For others, however, learning disorders don't become apparent until the middle school or high school years. By this point, schoolwork has become more demanding. Students who were able to get by in elementary school may no longer be able to mask their learning difficulties.

About 15–35% of children and teens with ADHD meet federal and state criteria for a learning disability. This combination of conditions can make school very challenging, even for the brightest students. ADHD and learning disorders each affect the ability to acquire and use new information. Taken together, they may lead to constant struggles and repeated failures at school. These negative experiences, in turn, may foster pessimism and low self-esteem. In that frame of mind, it's even harder for teens to find the motivation to do their best academically. To break out of this cycle, teens with ADHD and learning disorders need appropriate help for both conditions.

Substance Abuse

Adolescents with ADHD are more likely than their peers of the same age and sex to drink alcohol or abuse drugs. They also tend to start using these substances at an earlier age. Plus, they have an increased risk of developing alcoholism and drug addiction, especially if they also meet the criteria for conduct disorder.

Smoking follows a similar pattern: Adolescents with ADHD are more likely than those without ADHD to start smoking at a young age, and they have a tougher time quitting. The risk of becoming a daily smoker by age 17 is nearly twice as high in young people with ADHD, compared to peers without the condition.

Some teens with ADHD may turn to alcohol, drugs or smoking in an attempt to self-medicate, whether they're consciously aware of this motive or not. They may be looking to soothe ADHD symptoms or ease anxiety and self-consciousness about feeling different. Other teens may drink, use drugs, or smoke as part of a larger pattern of troubled behavior. Having a condition such as conduct disorder along with ADHD increases the risk for substance abuse.

A problem with drinking or drugs can seriously undermine a teen's overall mental and physical health. School performance and social relationships are concerns for many teens with ADHD, and alcohol and drugs only multiply the challenges. Also, the risk of getting into a traffic accident or sustaining other injuries is already higher among youth with ADHD than it is for those without it, and alcohol and drugs greatly increase those dangers. If your child has a drinking or drug problem, professional treatment can help. And if your child needs to quit smoking, there are programs and products to help with that as well.

Tics and Tourette Syndrome

Young people with ADHD are more likely than peers without ADHD to develop tics—sudden, rapid, repetitive movements or vocalizations. Teens with tics have little or no control over them. The tics may take a variety of forms, such as excessive eye blinking, throat clearing, sniffing, grunting, shoulder shrugging, or yelling out words. Tourette syndrome is a more severe tic disorder, in which movement and vocal tics generally occur many times throughout the day.

When tics and ADHD are found together, the ADHD usually starts two to three years before the tics. Tic disorders are often associated with obsessive and compulsive tendencies and increased anxiety in addition to ADHD.

In most young people with ADHD, stimulant medication doesn't increase tics and may actually decrease tic symptoms. Occasionally, however, stimulant medication used to treat ADHD may bring out or slightly worsen tics in young people who are already prone to them. If necessary, the doctor may lower the stimulant dose or switch to a non-stimulant medication. Tics that begin in childhood sometimes lessen on their own by adolescence. Often, if the tics continue at all, they may be so mild that they cause no significant problems and require no specific treatment. However, some teens have tics that are more severe and cause distress, interfere with school, or lead to problems in social situations. If needed, behavioral treatments and medications are available to treat tics.

The ADHD–Obesity Connection

The risk of obesity is increased by about 40% in children and teens with ADHD. There are several possible reasons for this:

- Inattention may contribute to failure to recognize and respond to internal cues about when they've consumed too much food.
- ADHD often goes hand in hand with poor planning and self-regulation skills. This may make it harder to plan an eating and exercise schedule, make healthy diet choices, and stick with regular meal and exercise times.
- Lack of enough sleep is a common issue for teens with ADHD. Research has shown that the less sleep teens get, the more likely they are to become overweight or obese.

Although more research is needed, there's evidence that the risk of obesity may be lower when ADHD is treated with medication. In addition, behavioral strategies for managing ADHD can help teens establish healthy routines for eating, exercising, and sleeping. This type of overall healthy lifestyle plays a key role in weight control.

ADHD Causes and Risk Factors

As the parent of an adolescent with ADHD, you've probably wondered at some point: *Why my child?* There's no single, simple answer to that question. In most cases, the cause of ADHD seems to be neither genes alone nor the environment alone, but an interaction of the two.

ADHD often runs in families. In fact, twin and family studies show that about three-fourths of the variability in ADHD occurrence can be accounted for by genes. It's estimated that the sibling of a child with ADHD has about a 20% chance of also having ADHD. There is about a 40% chance that at least one biological parent of a child with ADHD also has the condition.

For several years, researchers have been attempting to pinpoint exactly which genes are involved. Much remains to be learned, but what's known is that there is not a single, all-powerful "ADHD gene." Instead, ADHD appears to arise from a variation in one or more genes acting in concert with other genes. There are numerous pathways—perhaps hundreds or thousands of them—that can lead to ADHD.

Some genetic variants are inherited, accounting for the tendency of ADHD to be passed down through families. But other genetic variants are acquired through permanent changes in genes that occur in the womb or at any time after birth. Such changes may be caused by harmful environmental agents, such as tobacco smoke or prolonged exposure to lead.

Gene Expression

An individual with one or more specific genetic variants may have the potential to develop ADHD. But that potential may only be activated when conditions are ripe inside body cells, where genetic information is put to work.

Gene expression is the technical term for the process by which the information encoded in one of these genes is used to direct the production of a protein in a cell. Proteins are needed for the structure and regulation of every tissue and organ in the body, including the brain. So the expression of certain genes affects the brain, and the brain influences behavior.

But what affects conditions inside the cell? It turns out that environmental factors—for example, nutrition, sleep, exercise, and stress—influence the cellular milieu in which genes are expressed. And these, in turn, affect gene expression, which affects brain function, which influences behavior. Ultimately, nature and nurture come together inside cells, and sometimes the outcome is an adolescent with ADHD.

The *DRD4* Gene and Attention

Numerous genetic variants are thought to play a role in the development of ADHD. One of the best studied is a particular version of the dopamine D$_4$ receptor (*DRD4*) gene. Research conducted at the National Institutes of Health showed that children who carry this *DRD4* variant tend to have thinner brain tissue in the part of the brain linked to attention.

This study also provided insight into why some children's ADHD symptoms lessen in adolescence. Children in the study were followed for six years, from late childhood into their teens. As they grew up, their brains continued developing until they reached normal thickness in the affected area, and their ADHD symptoms improved as well. However, the *DRD4* variant is just one of a large number of factors that may be involved in causing and perpetuating ADHD, which helps explain why ADHD usually doesn't fade away completely.

Trauma and Chronic Stress

Several environmental factors have been studied in relationship to ADHD. Some of the most compelling evidence shows a link between ADHD and trauma or chronic stress. Both trauma and prolonged stress can have lingering effects on a person, psychologically and physiologically. The impact can reach all the way down to the cellular level. The effects of trauma and stress alone may not cause ADHD. But combined with other environmental and genetic factors, they may exacerbate ADHD symptoms in someone who is already prone to the condition.

Young people who experience trauma and abuse are at heightened risk for having ADHD. The reason for this association is still being explored. It's likely that trauma and abuse may bring out or worsen ADHD symptoms in susceptible teens.

But the relationship cuts both ways: It's also likely that ADHD may increase the risk of suffering trauma or abuse in the first place. For example, a teen who frequently aggravates classmates by butting into their conversations and bouncing off the walls may be at risk for physical bullying. A teen who impulsively gets into the car with a stranger may be at risk for sexual assault.

Something similar is thought to occur with chronic stress. Research shows that young people who grow up under stressful circumstances tend to have increased problems with ADHD. Ongoing sources of stress—such as parental alcoholism, family conflict, and multiple foster placements—may bring out ADHD or make it worse in some teens. But once again, this is a two-way street: Having a teen with ADHD in the family may also add to the general level of stress, discord, and chaos at home.

Keep in mind that there's a positive side to the story. If chronic stress worsens ADHD, then helping your teen *reduce* chronic stress should lessen its toll. Just offering your support can make a huge difference. Talk about how following a management plan for ADHD helps cut back on distress related to the condition. Then discuss how to face any stress and challenges that remain without freaking out or feeling overwhelmed and become a good role model and coach for the strategies you discuss. You'll find tips about how to do this sprinkled throughout the pages to come. A therapist may be able to provide more individualized suggestions.

More Risk Factors

Researchers have also looked at a number of other factors that may contribute to ADHD. The likely culprits include the following:

- Prenatal and birth factors. Mothers who smoked or drank alcohol during pregnancy are more likely to have children with ADHD symptoms. Premature birth and low birth weight are also associated with an increased risk for ADHD.
- Lead poisoning. Exposure to lead—for example, from paint or plumbing in older homes—may result in hyperactivity and difficulty concentrating. Children exposed to lead in early childhood are especially vulnerable to its lasting effects.
- Traumatic brain injury. Young people who have sustained brain injuries, such as concussions, may show ADHD-like behaviors afterward. However, a majority of children and teens with ADHD do not have a history of traumatic brain injury.

Causes of Comorbidity

Why do some teens end up having not only ADHD but also another emotional, behavioral, or learning disorder? In many cases, the answer lies in shared genetic and environmental factors.

There's a surprisingly large amount of overlap in genetic risk between ADHD and other mental health disorders. A study by the Psychiatric Genomics Consortium revealed that 28% of the variability in ADHD occurrence can be traced to genetic factors that are shared with several mental health conditions, including major depression.

Some environmental risk factors cast a wide net, too. For example, trauma and chronic stress may play a role not only in ADHD but also in conditions such as depression, conduct disorder, and substance abuse.

In other cases, comorbid conditions are actually a direct result of ADHD that isn't managed as well as it could be. For example, let's say a child with ADHD is constantly being punished by parents and singled out as a problem by teachers. Over time, the child may grow into an angry, uncooperative teen who sees adults as enemies, and that may lay the groundwork for ODD.

At the same time, a child whose ADHD is not well managed may experience a lot of failure in school, frustration in after-school activities, and rejection by peers. By adolescence, the child's self-esteem may be in tatters, and that may set the stage for depression.

The Perils of Letting Go Too Soon

As a parent, you already have a lot on your plate. It can be tempting to hope that your child's ADHD will just work itself out over time. The hands-off approach may seem especially alluring now that your child is older. Parenting a child with ADHD isn't easy, and fatigue can build up year after year after year. By this point, you may be feeling exhausted and burned out. And you may believe that it's time for your teen to start figuring things out on his or her own.

There might also be an element of denial at play. Admitting to yourself just how much your teen is struggling can sometimes be difficult. Yet ignoring the warning signs and refusing to face the realities of ADHD can be particularly risky during the adolescent years. Following are just a few of the possible consequences of unmanaged ADHD:

- Accidental injuries. Children and teens with ADHD have more frequent and severe injuries, on average, than their counterparts without ADHD. Inattention and impulsivity make them more likely to get into an accident as a pedestrian, while riding a bicycle, or while driving a car.
- Difficult peer relationships. Inattentive teens may be seen by their peers as standoffish, and hyperactive or impulsive teens may be seen as troublemakers. Such negative perceptions often lead to rejection. For one study, CDC researchers surveyed a nationally representative sample of parents about their children ages 4 to 17. Parents reported that children with a history of ADHD were 10 times as likely to have difficulties with friendships as children without ADHD.
- High-risk sex. Adolescents with ADHD are more likely than those without the condition to engage in risky sexual behavior. For example, they may have a history of multiple sex partners, or they may fail to use a condom consistently. Impulsivity, conduct disorder, and substance abuse may all play a role.
- Juvenile delinquency. Impulsivity can lead to making poor choices in other areas of life as well. This may result in trouble with the law, especially when coupled with conduct disorder. Youth with ADHD are three times more likely to be involved with the justice system, compared to their peers without ADHD.
- Dropping out of school. Students with ADHD are more likely than those without the condition to repeat a grade or drop out of high school. A study from the University

of California, Davis, found that about one-third of students with the combined form of ADHD failed to graduate high school on time—more than double the rate for students with no mental health disorder.

To help your teen avoid these perils, resist the urge to let go too soon. Adolescents with ADHD continue to need close monitoring and loving guidance. They also need parents who advocate for them at school and in the community. Being there for your teen takes time and energy. But the demands may feel less overwhelming once you've learned how to use some proven strategies and where to turn for assistance and support.

Staying Involved and Promoting Well-Being

The good news is that, just as there are factors that can worsen your child's ADHD symptoms, there are also factors that can promote well-being. By improving cellular health, these factors may even have a positive effect on the way genes are expressed.

Of all these beneficial factors, the relationship between parent and child is paramount. Teens thrive when they have a parent in their corner, and they benefit from an atmosphere of open, honest communication. Whether they are willing to admit it or not, teens like knowing they can turn to a parent for advice when they have a problem.

The strength and quality of other relationships matter as well. Key adults other than parents—such as extended family members, teachers, coaches, and youth group leaders—may have a positive impact on academic achievement and self-esteem. Support from caring adults may also reduce the risk for conduct problems, risky sexual behavior, and substance abuse.

Don't Forget to Nurture Yourself, Too

Throughout this book, we'll talk about ways you can help your adolescent with ADHD thrive. But it's hard to be there for someone else when you're feeling burned out and exhausted yourself. Put your parenting skills to good use, and nurture yourself as thoughtfully as you care for the rest of your family. Eat wisely, exercise regularly, and make sleep a priority. Keep working on the important relationships in your life, too.

If you have a partner in parenting—such as a spouse, an ex who shares custody, or your own parent who lends a hand—help each other out. Talk frankly about the stress involved in raising a teen with ADHD, and give each other breaks.

Many parents also appreciate the comradery they find in support groups for families of children and adolescents with ADHD. Ask your child's doctor or therapist about local groups, or check out the resources compiled by Children and Adults with Attention-Deficit/Hyperactivity Disorder (CHADD; chadd.org), a national membership organization that offers both in-person meetings and online support.

Developmental Assets

In 1990, a nonprofit organization called Search Institute (search-institute.org) first published a list of 40 Developmental Assets—a set of skills, experiences, relationships, and behaviors, grounded in scientific evidence, that help young people grow into successful, productive adults. The Developmental Assets framework has since been widely used to guide programs and research focused on positive aspects of youth development.

The Developmental Assets for adolescents fall into eight categories. These are examples of the kinds of things that help teens grow into healthy, responsible adults:

- Support—from family, other adults, caring neighbors, and school personnel
- Empowerment—through feeling valued, feeling safe, and giving back to the community

- Boundaries and expectations—via clear rules, high standards, and positive role models
- Constructive use of time—for creative hobbies, youth programs, and religious activities
- Commitment to learning—through engaging with school, doing homework, and reading
- Positive values—such as integrity, honesty, responsibility, and social justice
- Social competencies—such as friendship skills, cultural sensitivity, and the ability to resist negative peer pressure
- Positive identity—via empowerment, self-esteem, and optimism about the future

Having ADHD may make it tougher for teens to attain some of these skills, but not all of them. And getting treatment for ADHD can help teens work toward the skills that are more difficult, such as staying engaged with school and building friendships.

Looking Ahead to a Hopeful Future

You probably wonder what the future holds for your teen with ADHD. There will undoubtedly be challenges, but there will also be successes—and you can help tilt the balance more in the latter direction. The pages ahead are chock-full of information about helping your teen build on strengths and shore up weaknesses.

Adolescent ADHD can be treated with the right mix of behavioral therapy, medication, educational strategies, and community interventions. The symptoms of ADHD may not go away completely, but they can usually be kept to a more manageable level with appropriate treatment. Finding the best combination of approaches for your teen may take some time and effort. But you can help the process along by partnering with other caregivers, teachers, therapists, doctors, and, most importantly, your teen.

Key Points

- Your child's ADHD symptoms may change in adolescence. Inattention—difficulty with paying attention and staying mentally focused—often takes center stage.
- Getting a professional diagnosis is important if you suspect that your child has ADHD.
- Most adolescents with ADHD also have at least one other emotional, behavioral, or learning disorder, which multiplies the day-to-day challenges they face.
- Adolescents with ADHD are at increased risk for difficult relationships, conduct problems, substance abuse, risky sexual behavior, and dropping out of school.
- Appropriate support from caring adults—and especially a strong parent–child relationship—can lessen these risks and promote success in daily life.

Learn More

A good starting point for broad-based information and support is Children and Adults with Attention-Deficit/Hyperactivity Disorder (CHADD; chadd.org). Another excellent resource on attention and learning issues is Understood (understood.org), the collaborative effort of 15 nonprofit organizations. For an overview of the latest ADHD research and statistics, go to the Centers for Disease Control and Prevention website (cdc.gov/adhd).

Chapter Three

Finding the Best Treatment for Your Teen: Behavioral Approaches

Many people equate treatment for ADHD with medication. Over the years, there has been public debate about how to balance the benefits of drug therapy for children and teens with ADHD against the risk of side effects. That's a very important issue, and we'll discuss it at length in the next chapter. But what often gets lost in the discussion is that there are safe, effective, non-drug treatments for ADHD as well.

ADHD is a brain-based condition that affects attention and behavior, so it makes sense that behavioral therapy should play a role in managing it. For some adolescents with ADHD, behavioral therapy alone may suffice. If drug therapy is required, a combination of both medication and behavioral therapy is usually preferable to medication alone. In such cases, it's generally more effective to start with behavioral therapy and then add medication as needed.

Many people say they prefer combined treatment. In one study, more than 1,100 members of the general public were asked which treatment approach they believed to be best for kids with ADHD: counseling, medication, both, or neither.

About two-thirds said both. But among those who preferred only one treatment approach, counseling was chosen about four times as often as medication.

The widespread belief in the usefulness of non-drug treatments for ADHD is well founded. Behavioral treatments have much to recommend them:

- They don't carry the same risk of side effects as medication.
- They can address the emotional and social fallout of ADHD, such as low self-esteem and troubled relationships.
- They can help to promote successful academic performance.
- They can target other mental health conditions that often go along with ADHD, such as anxiety, depression, conduct problems, and substance abuse.
- They teach valuable skills that can be used for a lifetime.

Chris's Story

One thing that sets psychological and behavioral treatments apart from drug therapy is that the benefits may continue to be felt long after formal treatment has ended. In the case of Chris, now 17, his parents began taking him to see a psychologist the year he started middle school.

"This was an absolutely crucial time for Chris," recalls his mother, Lisa. "Part of the reason was related to ADHD. When he was younger, he was brutally bullied verbally for a while, and then the other kids just stopped paying attention to him at all. So by the time he got to sixth grade, he had a lot of social issues and low self-esteem to work out."

At the same time, Chris was going through puberty and discovering more about himself. "He figured out that he was gay," says Lisa. Dealing with emerging sexual and romantic feelings is something that all adolescents must deal with, regardless of sexual orientation. Having ADHD may make it more challenging to sort out these complicated feelings. Sexuality was another aspect of growing up that Chris talked about with his psychologist.

The psychologist visits continued off and on throughout middle school. "Then in his freshman year, the psychologist was like, 'You know, things are going pretty good. I'm sure I'll see you again, but let's take a break, and you can call me if you need me,'" Lisa says. "So far, we haven't needed to call."

Today, Chris still takes two medications to manage ADHD and anxiety, and he checks in every three months with the psychiatrist who prescribes them. In addition, he now travels two hours round trip daily to attend a high school that prides itself on accommodating the needs of students who learn differently. In this supportive environment, Lisa says, Chris is thriving, academically and socially.

At home, Lisa and Chris continue to use many of the strategies the psychologist taught them. "I would say a lot of what we do is maintenance and consistency—and figuring out how we can help Chris continue to do what he's supposed to do without making him feel like he's five years old," Lisa says.

As an example, she cites an ongoing struggle over the late-night use of electronic devices. "He would take the phone or tablet upstairs to bed with him, which meant he didn't go to sleep until 2 or 3 a.m.," says Lisa. And that meant he didn't want to get up at 5:45 the next morning for the long drive to school.

Now Lisa insists that he plug the phone and tablet into chargers on the kitchen counter at night. "It's a neutral location, but also a location where I'll notice right away if he sneaks them upstairs," Lisa says. She and Chris have talked about how staying up late playing games on his phone or watching a movie on his tablet leads to a miserable morning. Lisa has also pointed out that having the phone in the kitchen every morning makes it handy to put it in his backpack along with his lunch. Taking this approach hasn't completely ended conflicts over screen time, but it has reduced them.

"I've found that a lot of dealing with kids, whatever their ages, comes down to reasonable ideas," says Lisa. "But when you're in the thick of it, you can't always think of those practical things." At such times, the guidance of an expert can be invaluable.

Behavioral Therapy for ADHD

A variety of treatment approaches have been touted for ADHD in adolescents. However, the one with the strongest research base is behavioral therapy. This form of therapy focuses on identifying behaviors to change, taking steps to make it more likely that desired behaviors will occur, and providing appropriate consequences for behaviors. Although more research is needed, there is sufficient evidence to show that this approach generally works with adolescents who have ADHD.

There are activities you and your teen can do *before* a behavior occurs to stack the deck so that your child is more likely to behave appropriately. For example, you can model good listening and communication skills. You can also help your child set appropriate goals and make daily schedules. These are known as the *antecedents* of the behavior.

There are also things you can do *after* a behavior occurs that increase or decrease the likelihood that your child will act that way again. These are the *consequences* of the behavior. We'll return to the ABCs—antecedents, behaviors, and consequences—of behavior change further in this chapter.

Complementary Approaches to Managing ADHD

Both behavioral therapy and medication have been extensively studied in young people with ADHD. There's strong scientific evidence for their effectiveness, so they're considered first-line treatment options. If you enter "ADHD" into any online search engine, however, you'll instantly see that there are many, many other purported treatments that people are talking about.

Our goal for this book is to empower you with the best available information and most effective management strategies. Consequently, we've focused mainly on treatments with the strongest evidence base. However, we know that you may be curious about other options as well, so we've discussed several additional approaches at relevant points throughout the book. In each case, we've tried to briefly summarize what's known—and what isn't—about how well these approaches may work for managing ADHD symptoms. Here's where you'll find key topics:

- Neurofeedback: Chapter Three
- Executive function training: Chapter Three
- Meditation and yoga: Chapter Three
- Fatty acid supplements: Chapter Four
- Elimination diets: Chapter Five
- Physical exercise: Chapter Six

Some of these approaches have benefits for general health, but their effectiveness as an ADHD treatment is still unclear. Others have not yet been subjected to rigorous, large-scale research, or the findings have been mixed. In any case, these approaches are best used to supplement—not replace—treatments with proven effectiveness. To learn more about complementary approaches to managing ADHD, a good starting place is the National Center for Complementary and Integrative Health website (nccih.nih.gov/health/adhd).

How Behavioral Therapy Grows Up with Your Child

In younger children with ADHD, behavioral therapy relies primarily on the involvement of parents. The parents are taught how to use antecedents and consequences to promote more appropriate behavior. They do much of the direct work with the therapist, learning to set goals for their child's behavior and use rewards and punishments to nudge a target behavior in the right direction. If your child's ADHD was diagnosed and treated in preschool or elementary school, you may be familiar with this approach.

Once your child reaches the preteen and teen years, however, the involvement of your child takes on much greater importance. A five- or six-year-old has a lively mental life, but the capacity for self-reflection and planning is limited at that age. In contrast, a typical 15- or 16-year-old has developed a greater capacity to examine his or her own thoughts, reflect on the past, anticipate the future, and consider multiple options for behavior.

With professional guidance, an adolescent is able to play a bigger role in defining his or her own goals, planning how to reach them, and engaging in problem-solving to overcome barriers that get in the way. Expect that your teen will work more directly with the therapist. Actively involving a teen in behavioral therapy and getting buy-in to the process is important.

Just don't be surprised if your teen initially opposes getting involved in counseling. This is common. If that happens, it's best not to force the issue. You can still get some counseling and parent coaching on your own. The therapist can help you develop communication and negotiation skills and fine-tune your own parenting behaviors. Eventually, this may lead to your teen being more willing to take part in counseling, too.

Behavioral Strategies with Proven Benefits

Behavioral treatments for ADHD have been widely studied in children younger than 12. Much less research has been done in adolescents. Although that's starting to change, for now, most of what's known about treatment effectiveness is still based on studies conducted in younger children. When researchers from the University of Ohio, led by Dr. Steven Evans, reviewed published studies involving both children and teens with ADHD, they found solid scientific support for the four types of behavioral approaches discussed next.

Behavioral Family Interventions

As we've already seen, parents can learn to use behavioral strategies to help shape their children's behavior. With adolescents, it's important to also involve the teens themselves in the process, if possible. Teens may help set goals for therapy and learn strategies for making behavior changes. They may also learn skills that support behavior change, such as problem-solving and organizational skills. Plus, parents and teens may work together with a therapist to improve their relationship and hone their communication. More information about strategies for working with your child at home can be found in Chapter Five.

Behavioral Classroom Interventions

Behavioral principles can also be applied to managing behavior in the classroom. Teachers, like parents, can communicate and engage in problem-solving with teens to change antecedents and consequences in an intentional way. This can foster positive behavior and instill good learning and study habits. Typical target behaviors include completing in-class work, taking effective notes in class, coming prepared to class, following teacher instructions, and following classroom rules. More information about school-based strategies can be found in Chapter Seven.

Organizational Skills Training

This type of behavioral training focuses specifically on helping students learn to organize school materials, keep track of homework assignments, and manage homework and study time. For example, students might keep their papers organized in a binder or create a timeline for completing a big report. With teens, much of the focus is on developing self-management skills, which help them gradually assume more responsibility for getting their schoolwork done.

A prime example of organizational skills training is the Homework, Organization, and Planning Skills (HOPS) program, developed by Dr. Joshua Langberg and his colleagues. This program is designed for middle school students with ADHD. A school counselor or psychologist meets individually with students at school. There are about 16 meetings in all, each lasting no more than 20 minutes.

The program focuses on practical skills needed for academic success. For example, to better organize their materials, students are taught how to arrange their backpacks, binders, and lockers more efficiently. They also learn to consistently record homework assignments, class projects, and upcoming tests in a planner. To better manage their time, students are taught how to break down big school projects into smaller pieces and then plan for the completion of each piece. They also create an evening schedule that balances homework and study time with extracurricular activities.

In one study, middle school students with ADHD were randomly assigned to either take part in the HOPS program or be put on a waiting list. By the study's end, parents of students in the HOPS group reported greater improvement in organized actions, materials management, task planning, and homework completion. Most of these gains were still apparent three months later.

Combined Family–School Interventions

Of course, the ultimate goal is to help young people with ADHD succeed both at home *and* at school. Recognizing this fact, some of the most effective treatment programs have included a mix of family and classroom strategies. One such program is Family-School Success, developed by Dr. Power and his colleagues at the Perelman School of Medicine of the University of Pennsylvania and Children's Hospital of Philadelphia.

The Family-School Success program is designed for students in kindergarten through sixth grade with the inattentive or combined types of ADHD. Parents take part in six group training sessions along with other moms and dads. Kids participate in their own group meetings at the same time. The program also includes four family therapy sessions and two parent–teacher meetings.

A variety of behavioral strategies are used. In one called "daily report cards," teachers evaluate students on at least one target behavior every day and send home daily reports on how the students did. For their part, the parents learn to set reasonable goals for the target behaviors and provide appropriate rewards at home for meeting the goals.

A study of Family-School Success showed that it improved homework performance and strengthened parenting skills. It also led to greater family involvement in education and better collaboration between the family and the school.

Although this program was originally developed for sixth-grade and younger students, the same general approach could be adapted to older adolescents. With older students, it would be more important to involve the teens themselves in setting goals, developing and implementing organizational strategies, and evaluating consequences.

For example, an adaptation of daily report cards that's often used with teens is to have them evaluate their own performance at various intervals throughout the day. They then compare their ratings with those of teachers. Students can earn points or credits based on the extent to which their ratings match those of their teachers.

The focus of family therapy would also shift somewhat with older adolescents. A major focus of family therapy at this age is helping parents and teens learn to communicate, negotiate, and problem-solve effectively.

Summer Camps and After-School Programs

Annoying, immature, rude, bossy. These are just a few of the unflattering adjectives that other kids may use to describe adolescents with out-of-control ADHD.

Behavioral peer interventions are programs designed to reduce off-putting behaviors, build social skills, and promote more positive peer interactions. The programs bring together young people with ADHD and related conditions at summer camps or in weekend or after-school meetings. The agenda may include fun activities such as outdoor games, role playing, or podcasting. These activities give young participants a chance to make friends and be part of a group in a comfortable environment. They're surrounded by other youngsters who share similar interests and challenges, and they're supported by mentors and coaches who can guide their interactions.

For younger children, there's evidence that such programs can be helpful. Teens, however, face a whole new set of social challenges, such as making plans with friends independently of parents, resisting peer pressure, handling romantic rejection, and dealing with bullying on social media. Less is known about how well this type of program may work for adolescents with ADHD.

ABCs of Changing a Problem Behavior

Behavioral approaches can be used to address diverse behaviors in different settings. Yet all are rooted in a handful of basic techniques. Following is a quick rundown of techniques that have earned the scientific stamp of approval.

Laying the Groundwork

Your goal may be to help your teen get a handle on ADHD. But before the two of you are ready to tackle that challenge, you need to be able to work together effectively. The first order of business is creating and maintaining a strong parent–child relationship. These relationship-building strategies lay the foundation for success:

- Communication and negotiation. Clear communication allows you and your teen to share information, express opinions, and put feelings into words. Negotiation is the give-and-take of communication, helping you resolve an issue when the two of you don't see eye to eye. Examples of specific skills that you and your teen might need to work on include being a good listener, expressing yourself clearly, not monopolizing the conversation, and avoiding lecturing and blaming.
- Parental supervision. Now that your child is growing up and gaining more independence, you might feel as if your parenting job is done. The truth is, a teen needs your guidance and supervision. You can gradually loosen the reins as your child shows that he or she is ready for greater freedom and responsibility. But you should still stay involved in a developmentally appropriate way.

Managing Antecedents

Antecedents are things preceding a behavior that make it more likely to occur. By understanding and manipulating antecedents, you can stack the deck in favor of desirable behavior. These are some tried-and-true methods of managing antecedents:

- Goal setting. At home, you and your teen can work together to identify goals for your child's behavior. If the two of you are new to the process or have trouble agreeing on goals, input from a mental health professional is often helpful. The goals should be specific, realistic, and attainable in a reasonable amount of time. At school, your teen and a teacher may collaborate on goals for classroom behavior and academic performance.

- Action planning. Once you and your teen have identified goals, you need to devise a plan for putting them into action. Talk about when, where, and how your teen will enact the behavior. To help your teen stay on track, you may use prompts, such as posting a schedule on the fridge or setting a daily alarm on your teen's phone. Or you may establish a routine, such as always doing homework immediately after dinner.

- Behavioral contracts. Often, it helps to formalize your plan in a written behavioral contract. This is an agreement between you and your teen. It lays out which behaviors are being targeted for change and what the consequences of achieving or not achieving a behavioral goal will be. Behavioral contracts between a teacher and student may also be used in a school setting.

Managing Consequences

Consequences are things following a behavior that make it more or less likely to occur again. In psychology-speak, the process by which you change a behavior by modifying its consequences is called contingency management. You need to decide in advance which contingency management strategy to use and then apply it consistently. A mental health professional can help you choose the best strategy for a particular situation. These are the options at your disposal:

- Positive reinforcement. When a behavior is followed by something rewarding, it's more likely to be repeated. This is known as *positive reinforcement.* Your attention, approval, and praise are powerfully reinforcing. You could also set up a reward system in which your teen can earn an allowance or privileges by completing specified tasks.
- Negative reinforcement. When a behavior is followed by the removal of something unpleasant, it's also more likely to be repeated. This is known as *negative reinforcement.* For example, let's say you tell your teen to clean the bathroom. Your teen flips out, and you say, "Forget it; I'll do it myself." When you respond this way, your teen learns that flipping out is an effective way of avoiding something he or she doesn't want to do. This increases the chance that your teen will fly off the handle again when asked to do a chore. Of course, it's human nature to try getting out of disliked tasks. But adolescents with ADHD have a heavy dose of human nature, at least when it comes to avoiding tasks that are boring or require sustained attention. You need to be extra-vigilant to make sure you aren't inadvertently encouraging this kind of behavior with negative reinforcement.

- Strategic punishment. In general, positive reinforcement is a more effective tool for promoting behavior change than punishment. But for deterring serious rule infractions or unsafe behavior, an appropriate punishment, such as being grounded or losing privileges, may be in order. For punishment to be effective, make sure your teen understands how his or her behavior led to these consequences. Use punishment in a deliberate, judicious way and give your child much more positive reinforcement than punishment.

- Planned ignoring. One way to reduce or eliminate a less serious behavior problem is by making sure your teen doesn't receive attention for it. Attention of any kind—even annoyed or disapproving attention—can be a potent form of positive reinforcement. When you strategically refuse to offer attention for an unwanted behavior, the behavior will often get worse before it gets better. Eventually, however, it will start to fade away.

Fine-Tuning the Plan

Once you and your teen have put your behavioral plan into action, you need to monitor how well it's working. Then you can decide whether you need to make any adjustments. These are some strategies that can help with the fine-tuning:

- Self-monitoring. To determine whether your teen is meeting a stated goal, it's necessary to keep track of the target behavior. Teens can do much of this monitoring themselves. For example, let's say the target behavior is staying focused while doing homework. Your teen might set an alarm to beep every two minutes. Each time it beeps, your teen would then check "yes" or "no" on a checklist to indicate whether he or she is paying attention. Other behaviors might be tracked with a journal or on a chart. The information gleaned this way helps your teen see how much progress he or she has made over time, which can often be encouraging. If progress is lacking, that's a sign that you and your teen might need to adjust your plan.

- Problem-solving. Once your teen has made good progress toward changing a target behavior, it's time to start setting your sights on the next target. First, you and your teen identify another behavior that needs to be changed. Then, you consider alternative strategies that could be used. Finally, you start the process all over again, from setting goals and making plans to delivering consequences and monitoring progress.

Pros and Cons of Behavioral Approaches

Behavioral approaches to managing ADHD have a lot to recommend them. Numerous studies have shown that such approaches can reduce ADHD symptoms and lessen problems in daily life. For many young people, the effects of behavioral therapy may be equivalent to low-to-moderate doses of ADHD medication. The combination of behavioral therapy with low-dose medication may work as well as or better than a high dose of medication.

The benefits of these approaches go far beyond just improving attention or decreasing hyperactivity, however. Family interventions can improve your relationship with your teen, laying the groundwork for further changes. They make for a happier home life, not only for you and your teen, but also for other family members. A strong foundation at home, in turn, helps your teen to relate more effectively with peers and perform better in school.

Classroom interventions can boost your teen's academic performance and enhance the school experience. They make all those hours spent at school seem more successful and meaningful to your teen. That may translate into improved self-esteem as well as a more positive attitude toward getting a good education.

The core strategies learned in behaviorally based treatment can be applied to a wide range of life situations, including ones not directly related to ADHD. And unlike medication, which only works for as long as your teen keeps taking it, behavioral strategies may have long-lasting benefits. They can build skills, improve coping strategies, and shape habits of behavior that are helpful throughout adolescence and into adulthood.

The Flip Side

There may be limits to what such strategies can accomplish, however. Most adolescents with ADHD need medication in addition to behavioral treatment for the best results. There might be periods when everything seems to be smooth sailing, and you, your teen, and your teen's doctor decide to try a break from medication. But the majority of adolescents with ADHD continue to need medication much or all of the time.

An initial course of behavioral therapy may require 10 to 12 one-hour sessions in a therapist's office. To maintain the gains of treatment, periodic follow-up sessions are usually needed. Beyond that, for behavioral therapy to be effective, it is important to apply and practice the strategies on a daily basis. This requires more time and effort than simply handing out a pill, which may seem like a big disadvantage if your family has a busy schedule. Yet energy invested in your teen now may pay dividends for a lifetime.

Sometimes, everything goes along well for months or even years after the initial series of behavioral therapy sessions. Then, suddenly, your teen's symptoms flare up with a vengeance again. In such cases, you and your teen may need to return to the therapist for a brief series of sessions. This gives you a chance to explore what's going on and develop a plan for getting ADHD back under control.

Finding a Qualified Therapist

Behavioral strategies are relatively straightforward. Yet they can be difficult for people to use without some expert guidance, at least at the outset. The therapist who guides you may be a psychologist, child and adolescent psychiatrist, clinical social worker, or professional counselor.

Ideally, you're looking for a therapist who frequently works with adolescents, has expertise in behavioral therapy, and has experience treating ADHD. In addition, it's helpful to identify a therapist who is willing to collaborate with school professionals. Finding a therapist with that combination of attributes may not be easy, however, especially if you have limited financial resources or live outside a major metropolitan area.

Ask your child's primary care doctor for a referral, or contact your health insurance company to find mental health providers who are in your plan's network. You can also check the professional directory and the list of hospital and university ADHD centers on the Children and Adults with Attention-Deficit/Hyperactivity Disorder (CHADD) website (chadd. org). Or you can search the directory of therapists provided by the Association for Behavioral and Cognitive Therapies (findcbt.org).

Key Questions to Ask

To decide whether a therapist offers the type of services your teen requires, these are some questions you may want to ask:

- *How experienced are you at working with adolescents who have ADHD?* Look for a therapist whose background and experience are a good match for your teen's needs.
- *What therapeutic approach do you use for treating ADHD?* You are looking for an expert in behavioral treatment. Therapists who provide this type of treatment may refer to what they do as behavioral therapy or solution-focused therapy. Sometimes they may refer to their approach as cognitive-behavioral therapy, which is fine as long as they place a strong emphasis on using behavioral approaches. Keep in mind that the word *behavior* is found in the names of other types of therapy as well.
- *Will you work with my child alone, me alone, or both of us at once?* The best answer is "all of the above." Let's say your family embarks on an initial course of family behavioral therapy for 10 sessions or so. In a typical scenario, about one-third of the time in therapy would involve your teen meeting one-on-one with the therapist. This gives your teen a chance to start developing goals, engaging in problem-solving, and improving communication skills. About one-third of the sessions would involve you meeting with the therapist. This gives you an opportunity to learn some behavior management strategies and hone your own communication skills. And about one-third of the time would involve you and your teen seeing the

therapist together. This allows the two of you to do more work on communication, negotiation, and collaborative problem-solving. Some of the time may be devoted to creating a behavioral contract.

- *Are you willing to involve my child's school in the behavior management plan?* It's helpful if you and your child's teachers are on the same page. Look for a therapist who plans to communicate regularly with school personnel. In some cases, the therapist may even be willing to visit the school to observe your teen in class or meet with teachers.

- *Can you treat any other mental health or substance abuse disorders that my child may have?* A therapist who does not have training and expertise in treating a coexisting disorder should refer you to a qualified treatment provider. The therapist should be willing to coordinate care with the other provider to make sure your teen's overall treatment plan is cohesive.

ADHD Coaches and Your Teen's Game Plan

ADHD coaches are professionals who help clients with ADHD stay focused on their goals, stick with their plans, manage their time, and prioritize their activities. Coaching is meant to complement, not replace, therapy and medication. Many teens find that coaching is an invaluable tool for helping them keep their behavior on track.

Consider Ethan, for example. He began working with an ADHD coach soon after starting classes at a community college. "If Ethan had a paper due two weeks down the road, his coach would help him break it down into manageable steps," says his mother. "So it might be: Read pages 1–20 on Monday, read pages 21–40 on Tuesday, and on like that. Then the coach would check in to prompt him to do whatever he needed to be doing."

If you're considering hiring an ADHD coach for your teen, try to interview at least two or three candidates. Ask about their training, experience, and approach. Discuss whether the coach will work with your teen in face-to-face meetings or by video chat, phone, text, or email. Some coaches offer a complimentary session, which gives you a chance to gauge how well your teen clicks with the coach's approach and personality. Inquire about fees, and keep in mind that health insurance generally won't cover them.

Insurance Issues

Insurance coverage for mental and behavioral health services has expanded in recent years. Yet accessing such services may still be difficult in many cases, and finding out exactly what's covered by your family's health plan may take some detective work. Here are some key laws and programs to know about:

- Large-employer health plans. For most large-employer health plans, if mental health or substance abuse services are offered, they are subject to the requirements of the *Mental Health Parity and Addiction Equity Act.* Under this federal law, health plans generally cannot impose restrictions on mental health benefits that are less favorable than those imposed on medical and surgical benefits.
- Small-employer and individual health plans. The *Affordable Care Act* is a federal health care reform law, also known as Obamacare. Under this law, most small-employer and individual plans, including those offered through the Health Insurance Marketplace (healthcare. gov), must cover mental health and substance abuse services. (As this book was being written, the future direction of federal health care law was the subject of active political debate.)

- Medicaid and Children's Health Insurance Program (CHIP). Medicaid is a joint state–federal program that provides health care to individuals and families of modest means who meet eligibility requirements. CHIP extends health coverage to eligible uninsured children up to age 19 whose families have incomes too high for Medicaid. All state Medicaid programs provide some mental health services, and some provide substance abuse services, too. CHIP programs often provide an array of such services as well. To find out whether your child qualifies for free or low-cost health care through one of these programs, visit insurekidsnow.gov or call (877) KIDS-NOW (543-7669).

These laws and programs offer broad protections. However, the specific details of a health plan's coverage can vary widely from state to state and from plan to plan. Check your plan's Summary of Benefits and Coverage for information about mental health, behavioral health, and substance abuse benefits. Contact the plan directly if you're unsure whether a certain mental health care provider is part of your network or whether a particular diagnosis, assessment, treatment, or service is covered under your plan.

Be aware that a sizable number of psychologists, psychiatrists, and other mental health professionals don't take insurance, even if you have it. One study published in *JAMA Psychiatry* in 2014 found that private insurance was accepted by just over half of psychiatrists (medical doctors who specialize in mental health), compared to nearly 90% of physicians in other specialties.

Before making an appointment, ask whether the mental health care provider you're considering accepts your family's insurance. Also, when choosing a family health plan during the enrollment period, compare the mental health care providers in each plan's network and take that into account when making your selection.

Teaming Up with Your Teen's Therapist

Your teen is the one with ADHD. Yet when using behavioral approaches, you're an active participant in the treatment process. You'll probably be asked to attend many of the therapy sessions.

Parents take part in ADHD therapy in two main ways. You (and your partner, if any) may meet individually with the therapist to sharpen your own communication, relationship-building, and behavior management skills. This is referred to as *parent training*. Also, you and your teen (and perhaps your partner or, occasionally, your other children) may meet jointly with the therapist to work on shared behavioral and relationship goals. This is referred to as *family therapy*.

Why might you need parent training and family therapy at this stage in the game? As the parent of an adolescent, you have more than a decade of child-rearing under your belt. You may feel as if you're already pretty good at it—and you may be right. The fact that you are reading this book suggests that you're a dedicated, motivated parent. For adolescents whose attention and behavior are well regulated and whose academic skills are on track, you might already be doing more than enough to raise a happy, healthy teen.

For adolescents with ADHD, however, pretty good parenting isn't good enough. You need to shoot for excellence. Just as in other jobs, when you're aiming for the top of your field, you may need to undertake advanced training.

That's where a therapist can be helpful. The therapist can help you learn new parenting skills and dust off old ones that may have fallen into disuse. At the same time, a sensitive therapist can help you learn to forgive yourself when you fall short of excellence, because even an expert parent has an off day now and then.

Other Potentially Promising Strategies

Behavioral treatments for ADHD have solid research support. Some other psychological and behavioral approaches also show promise, based on limited studies. These approaches are worth keeping an eye on. However, more research is needed to establish their usefulness for helping adolescents manage ADHD.

Neurofeedback

Neurofeedback measures the electrical activity inside a person's brain and gives the person real-time information about it. The goal is to train the person so that he or she gains some voluntary control over this normally automatic brain activity.

During neurofeedback, electrical activity within the brain is measured using an electroencephalogram (EEG). Small, metal disks, called *electrodes*, are placed on the scalp. The electrodes pick up electrical signals from the brain and send them over attached wires to a recording device. The device then translates the signals into patterns of electrical activity, called *brain waves*. It's known that certain brain-wave patterns are associated with mental focus.

In a typical neurofeedback session, a teen might wear a cap lined with EEG electrodes while playing a special computer game. To control the action on the screen, the teen must produce a particular type of brain-wave activity in key areas of the brain. The teen uses brain waves produced by concentrated attention in place of a keyboard, mouse, or joystick to rack up points in the game.

Theoretically, this type of neurofeedback might help a teen learn to control specific brain waves in order to sharpen mental focus and thereby decrease problems in daily life. Studies to date suggest that neurofeedback may indeed affect attention to some extent, and it may even lead to sustained changes in brain functioning. But it's still unclear whether these changes boost performance in real-world situations, such as listening in class or studying for a test.

Neurofeedback training requires 30 to 40 sessions, compared to 10 to 12 for behavioral therapy. It can get quite expensive. And at this point, the most that can be said is that neurofeedback may possibly be effective for treating adolescent ADHD. Large-scale research now in progress will tell us more about how well neurofeedback works.

Do Meditation and Yoga Help?

Practicing meditation or doing yoga on a regular basis helps calm the mind, relax the body, ease tension, and enhance well-being. That's reason enough for teens with a condition as stressful as ADHD to consider giving these approaches a try.

A handful of small, preliminary studies have suggested that meditation and yoga might also help improve attention in children and teens with ADHD. However, larger, more rigorously controlled studies are needed to explore this possibility. For now, the National Center for Complementary and Integrative Health says that these approaches haven't been conclusively shown to reduce inattention in kids with ADHD.

Nevertheless, learning healthy ways to manage stress and promote a sense of well-being is important for everyone. For a teen who's interested in these approaches, there is little risk involved in trying meditation. If your teen wants to take a yoga class, look for a well-trained, experienced instructor. If your teen has any health conditions that may limit the ability to perform yoga moves, be sure to let the instructor know.

Executive Function Training

The frontal lobes are parts of each half of the brain, located behind the forehead, that are involved in cognitive activities and motor control. The front part of the frontal lobes, called the *prefrontal cortex*, plays an especially important role in executive functioning—the brain processes involved in organizing information, planning future actions, and regulating behavior and emotions. In young people with ADHD, brain scans show that the frontal and prefrontal regions of the brain tend to be under-active when performing activities that require sustained attention and effort.

ADHD medication may partially correct this underactivation, at least temporarily. However, some brain processes, such as working memory, may still be impaired. One reason is that key areas in the prefrontal cortex tend to develop more slowly than normal in young people with ADHD. In general, there is about a three-year lag in the development of these critical brain areas. Although medication can activate the areas, it doesn't appear that it makes them grow faster.

Executive function training—also called *brain training* or *cognitive training*—aims to address this limitation. It uses computer-based activities involving extensive repetition and practice to strengthen specific executive functioning skills. For example, some training programs are intended to target working memory. This is a limited-capacity brain system for temporarily holding and manipulating information, much like the clipboard on a computer.

Research indicates that more than four out of five young people with ADHD have deficits in specific aspects of working memory. For instance, they might have trouble working with certain facts while simultaneously holding other information in mind. Or they might allow too many irrelevant thoughts to compete for the limited space in working memory.

Using clever computer games to shore up these weaknesses is an appealing idea. So far, however, the approach is still experimental. A review of published research concluded that many existing training programs have design flaws limiting their effectiveness. Some fail to zero in on elements of working memory and executive functioning that are most affected by ADHD. At present, claims about improved grades or reduced ADHD symptoms are largely unsubstantiated. But it's possible this will change as the training programs become more sophisticated.

Combining Therapy and Medication

The gold standard for treating adolescent ADHD is behavioral therapy, medication, or both. If you're considering other approaches, such as neurofeedback or executive function training, they're probably best used in addition to—not in place of—these established treatments.

For many teens, a combination of behavioral therapy and medication is optimal. Double-teaming ADHD with both treatments may mean juggling multiple providers and higher costs for a while. Over a period of years, however, it might turn out to be more cost-effective than either treatment alone if it leads to better long-term management of ADHD with fewer side effects. Research suggests that the combined approach may be particularly beneficial for young people with both ADHD and another mental health condition, such as an anxiety disorder or depression.

Key Points

- Behavioral therapy focuses on identifying behaviors to change, providing positive reinforcement to make it more likely that desired behaviors will occur and using planned ignoring and strategic punishment to reduce undesired behaviors.
- Adolescents may get negative reinforcement by avoiding work. Behavioral therapy helps families understand how to deal effectively with these situations.
- You and your teen can stack the deck in favor of a desired behavior through effective communication, goal setting, action planning, and behavioral contracts.
- Behavioral approaches can reduce ADHD symptoms and lessen problems in daily life. They can also promote success at school and target other mental or behavioral health issues.
- Most adolescents with ADHD benefit from medication in addition to behavioral treatment.

Learn More

For further information, including what to expect from therapy and where to find a therapist, visit the Association for Behavioral and Cognitive Therapies website (abct.org). Another great resource on evidence-based mental health treatment for adolescents is the Society of Clinical Child and Adolescent Psychology (effectivechildtherapy.org).

Chapter Four

Finding the Best Treatment for Your Teen: ADHD Medications

Many adolescents with ADHD have been taking medication since elementary school. If that's true for your family, you may already have a lot of experience with one or more of the drugs used to treat ADHD. By now, you and your teen's doctor may have identified the medication regimen that works best for your child with the fewest side effects. If you're lucky, your teen may even have noticed how much the medication helps and is willing to keep taking it.

Just bear in mind that the one constant in child development is change—and that's never more true than during adolescence. This is a time of rapid transition for your child, physically, mentally, and behaviorally. It's also a period when coexisting conditions—such as depression, anxiety, oppositional defiant disorder (ODD), and conduct disorder—may be getting worse. In some cases, your teen's ADHD symptoms may no longer respond to the same medication, dose, and dosage schedule that worked out well before.

In other cases, your or your child's view of medication may have evolved over time. Teens may start questioning why they need to take medication. Parents may begin worrying about the potential for teens to abuse certain drugs or to sell or give away medication to friends. Meanwhile, household routines and parental supervision, which can help ensure that medication is used properly, might be getting laxer as teens become more independent.

The bottom line: You and your teen may still have some significant challenges ahead, whether your child is brand new to ADHD medication, is resuming it after a break, or has been taking it for years. But don't let that discourage you.

Medication is an integral part of treatment for many adolescents with ADHD. Initially, you'll need to work closely with the doctor to find the best medication or combination of medications for your child. After that, your teen will need periodic follow-up appointments to make sure the prescribed treatment is still on track. In addition, medication should be just one part of a broader ADHD management plan, which also includes evidence-based family behavioral therapy, organizational and social skills training, and classroom strategies at school.

When you make sure those things happen, the odds are in your teen's favor. For the large majority of adolescents with ADHD who take medication, doctors are able to find a medication regimen that reduces their symptoms with minimal side effects.

Joe's Story

Kids with ADHD often start taking medication at an early age, but that's not always true. In Joe's case, his parents were hesitant to use medication because of their strong commitment to leading a natural lifestyle. In particular, his father, a chiropractor, preferred to try non-drug options first and use medication only as a last resort.

By sophomore year in high school, however, it was increasingly obvious that Joe was struggling. "He's very bright, but he failed some classes," his mother, Heather, recalls. "He couldn't juggle all the classes and the homework and the deadlines." At the same time, she says, "Life at home with Joe was becoming very chaotic. It put tremendous strain on our family."

Joe's concerned parents tried to help him with a variety of non-drug approaches, but it seemed clear that something more needed to be done. "We finally decided to go down the road of medication," says Heather. "But with the first medication the doctor prescribed, Joe had a lot of headaches and stomach aches." Alarmed, his parents soon stopped filling the prescription.

Meanwhile, the family was working with Joe's high school on classroom accommodations. One day, Heather had an eye-opening chat with the school psychologist. "She was able to explain to me that finding the right medication is a process," Heather recalls. "She helped me have a better idea about what to expect, and that encouraged us to try again."

This time around, the doctor prescribed a different drug. Joe was able to take it without troublesome side effects, but he said that he didn't think it was having positive effects either. It was a different story when Heather and Joe met with school staff, however. "They went around the room, and all the teachers and the principal said they saw a marked difference in my son," Heather says. "Joe just sat there and took it in. Later that night, he said, 'You know what, Mom? I asked my friends if they've noticed a difference, and they said they did, too.' I think he began seeing himself in a whole new light that day."

Joe, once on the verge of dropping out, went on to graduate from high school. Today, at age 18, he's living at home, taking three classes at a community college, and working part-time at a supermarket. And yes, he's still choosing to take medication for ADHD. "He's figuring out how to manage his schedule, including using mass transit to get to school and back," says Heather. "I think he might need to cut back his work hours. But he's getting good grades and doing well. I'm really proud of how far he has come."

Stimulant Medications for ADHD

The medications used to treat ADHD can be divided into two broad categories: stimulants and non-stimulants. As their name implies, stimulants tend to rev up attention, alertness, and energy. It might seem counterintuitive to give a stimulant to someone who is already bouncing off the walls. But for many people with ADHD, stimulants have a calming effect, increasing attentiveness while decreasing hyperactivity and impulsivity.

How is that possible? Dopamine and norepinephrine, two chemical messengers in the brain, are thought to play key roles. Research suggests that abnormalities in dopamine and norepinephrine activity within the brain are involved in causing the attentional and behavioral symptoms of ADHD. By affecting the activity of these brain chemicals, stimulants may improve attention, concentration, self-control, and executive functioning. They may also reduce hyperactive and impulsive behavior.

Stimulants have been a mainstay of ADHD treatment for decades. They are the best studied and most effective class of

ADHD medication. As a result, they're also the most widely prescribed. The number of prescriptions for stimulants that are written for adolescents with ADHD has risen sharply in recent years. That's likely due to increased awareness that, although ADHD may change, it usually doesn't go away when a child gets older.

Stimulants are sold under a variety of brand names (see Table 4.1). Many are capsules or tablets. For teens who have trouble swallowing pills, however, there are liquid syrups, a chewable tablet, and an orally disintegrating tablet (a type of pill designed for dissolving in a person's mouth rather than being swallowed whole). There is also a medicated patch available, which is worn on the skin of the hip (see Table 4.2).

Types of Stimulants

Stimulant medications approved by the U.S. Food and Drug Administration (FDA) for treating ADHD can be divided into two groups, based on their chemical makeup.

AMPHETAMINE COMPOUNDS
- Amphetamine (Adzenys XR-ODT, Dyanavel XR, Evekeo)
- Amphetamine and dextroamphetamine (Adderall, Adderall XR)
- Dextroamphetamine (Dexedrine Spansule, ProCentra, Zenzedi)
- Lisdexamfetamine (Vyvanse)

METHYLPHENIDATE COMPOUNDS
- Dexmethylphenidate (Focalin, Focalin XR)
- Methylphenidate (Aptensio XR, Concerta, Daytrana, Metadate CD, Methylin Chewable Tablets, Methylin ER, Methylin Oral Solution, Quillivant XR, Ritalin, Ritalin LA, Ritalin SR)

Table 4.1
ADHD Medications

Generic Name	Brand Name
Stimulants: Long Acting	
amphetamine	Adzenys XR-ODT
	Dyanavel XR
amphetamine and dextroamphetamine	Adderall XR
dexmethylphenidate	Focalin XR
dextroamphetamine	Dexedrine Spansule
lisdexamfetamine	Vyvanse
methylphenidate	Aptensio XR
	Concerta
	Daytrana
	Metadate CD
	Methylin ER
	Quillivant XR
	Ritalin LA
	Ritalin SR
Stimulants: Short Acting	
amphetamine	Evekeo
amphetamine and dextroamphetamine	Adderall
dexmethylphenidate	Focalin
dextroamphetamine	ProCentra
	Zenzedi
methylphenidate	Methylin Chewable Tablets
	Methylin Oral Solution
	Ritalin
Non-stimulants	
atomoxetine	Strattera
clonidine, extended release	Kapvay
guanfacine, extended release	Intuniv

All of these medications are FDA approved for the treatment of ADHD in children, and most are approved for adolescents as well.

Table 4.2
Alternatives to Swallowing a Pill

Form	Brand Name
Chewable tablet	Methylin Chewable Tablets
Liquid	Dyanavel XR
	Methylin Oral Solution
	ProCentra
	Quillivant XR
Orally disintegrating tablet	Adzenys XR-ODT
Patch	Daytrana

In general, all the stimulants are about equally effective. For a particular person, however, one may work better than another. In many cases, teens who don't respond well to a particular stimulant medication may respond better to another medication within the same group. In other cases, teens who fail to improve on an amphetamine compound may have a good response to a methylphenidate compound, and vice versa.

Timing Is Everything

Stimulants also differ in how long they are active in the body. That's a plus, because it enables the doctor to tailor the treatment to your teen's needs (see Table 4.1).

LONG-ACTING STIMULANTS

Today, doctors most often prescribe one of the stimulants with relatively long-lasting effects (see Table 4.1), which can often be taken just once a day. You'll see some of these medications designated as long acting (LA), extended release (XR or ER), or sustained release (SR). The exact duration of the effects can vary from medication to medication and from person to person. Generally speaking, however, the effects last for 6 to 12 hours.

Let's say a teen takes a long-lasting stimulant at 7:30 a.m. before leaving for school. If the effects last about 10 hours, the medication will keep working until around 5:30 p.m. This gets the teen through the whole school day, which may be all that's necessary. In fact, having the medication wear off in the late afternoon might be a good thing, if it helps curb evening side effects such as lack of appetite and trouble sleeping.

The methylphenidate patch is a special case. Its effects take longer to kick in—about two hours versus 20 to 60 minutes for oral stimulants. Therefore, to provide coverage for the entire school day, the patch must be applied a couple of hours before school starts—a time when many teens would much rather be tucked in bed sleeping. Once the patch begins working, the effects last for up to 10 hours if it's worn for the recommended maximum time. If the patch is removed early, the effect will continue for about one to two hours after removal.

SHORT-ACTING STIMULANTS

Some teens need their medication to last a bit longer into the evening. For example, medication might help them complete their homework, study for a test, focus at sports practice, or perform an after-school job. In such cases, doctors will often prescribe a shorter-lasting stimulant to be taken later in the day. These medications are often referred to as *short acting* or *immediate release*. Typically, the effects last about four to five hours.

A commonly used approach is for teens to take a long-acting stimulant in the morning and a short-acting stimulant in the afternoon. Another approach is for teens to take a short-acting stimulant two or three times per day instead of (rather than in addition to) a longer-acting medication.

Stimulants: Pros and Cons

As a treatment for ADHD, stimulants have a long track record. A large body of research shows that these medications can help reduce inattention, hyperactivity, and impulsivity in many children and teens with ADHD. And that, in turn, may reduce many of the problems associated with ADHD, including academic underachievement, peer relationship problems, family conflict, and low self-esteem.

For example, let's say a student with uncontrolled ADHD finds it hard to focus in school and often gets into trouble for disrupting class instead of listening to the teacher. The right medication may improve the student's attention and self-control at school, and that helps the student listen in class and take better notes—and perhaps resist the impulse to poke a classmate in the arm. As a result, the student may perform better academically and be more cooperative in class. There's also some evidence that taking medication may lead to higher self-esteem, probably because kids who get more positive feedback from teachers and peers feel better about themselves.

Compared to non-stimulant medications for treating ADHD, studies indicate that stimulants are generally more effective. And unlike their non-stimulant counterparts, stimulants can be started and stopped abruptly. This means that your teen can take the medication one day and not the next, which may come in handy if your teen only takes medication on school days or during the school year. But keep in mind that the symptoms and impairments caused by ADHD are likely to affect your teen not only at school but also at home, with friends, and in the community. As a result, many teens with ADHD need to keep taking their medication on the weekends and throughout the summer.

On the downside, about 20% to 30% of young people with ADHD don't respond to the first stimulant that's prescribed. Eventually, the doctor can usually find another stimulant or non-stimulant medication that will help. But at the outset, identifying the best medication for your teen may take some time and patience.

Even after a medication has been identified as effective, it's common for medication to work less effectively over time. Often, an adjustment in dose can address the concern, but sometimes a change in medication is needed. For this reason, ongoing monitoring in collaboration with the teen's doctor is critically important.

Stimulants: Side Effects and Safety Issues

Stimulant medications for ADHD are generally well tolerated, but side effects and complications sometimes occur. For many parents, the risk of adverse effects is a major cause for concern. When you're considering one of these medications, it's crucial to weigh the possible risks against the expected benefits in consultation with your teen's doctor.

Common side effects of stimulant medications include headaches, stomach aches, decreased appetite, and sleep problems. Often, such problems are mild and short-lived. But if your teen has side effects that are bothersome or don't go away, tell the doctor. In many cases, side effects can be minimized by finding the optimal dose and best time to take a medication. If that doesn't resolve the issue, the doctor may consider switching your teen to a different stimulant or non-stimulant drug.

The methylphenidate skin patch can cause the same side effects as oral forms of the same drug. In addition, some people develop skin redness, bumps, or itching at the site where the patch is applied. To minimize skin irritation, it can help to switch the place on the hip where the patch is applied.

Occasionally, more serious problems arise in teens who take stimulant medications. It's important for the doctor to evaluate your child's medical status and health risks before prescribing one of these drugs. Discuss these safety issues with your child's doctor:

- Potential for abuse. When taken in greater quantities or a different manner than prescribed, stimulants can be addictive. In addition, selling these medications or sharing them with others is a crime. Impress upon your teen the importance of using stimulant medications responsibly. Let the doctor know if your teen has a history of abusing drugs or alcohol.
- Heart health risks. Stimulants can slightly raise blood pressure and increase heart rate. Some evidence suggests that, in rare cases, these medications may be associated with sudden death in people who have pre-existing heart conditions or heart defects. It is important to tell your teen's health care professional if your child has a history of chest pain, shortness of breath, or fainting associated with exercise, or if your child develops these symptoms after starting the medication. Teens taking stimulant medications should have their blood pressure and heart rate checked periodically by a health care professional.
- Circulatory problems. Impaired circulation in the fingers and toes has also been reported in some individuals taking stimulant medications. Call the doctor if your teen develops any new numbness, pain, sensitivity to temperature, or change in skin color in the fingers or toes. Tell the doctor immediately if your teen develops

unexplained wounds on the fingers or toes while taking ADHD medication.

- Mental health problems. Sometimes, use of stimulants may trigger or worsen anxiety or depressive symptoms. If this occurs, discuss the situation with your teen's doctor. In very rare cases, use of stimulant medications may set off symptoms of psychosis (e.g., losing touch with reality, hearing voices, being paranoid) or mania (e.g., experiencing overly "up" moods, acting extremely euphoric or irritable). If your teen develops new or worsening symptoms such as these while taking ADHD medication, call the doctor right away.

- Growth delays. Although there is evidence that children's growth may slow down while taking stimulant medication, more recent research indicates that this problem is usually only temporary. Studies have shown that there were no differences in final adult height among teens who took stimulant medications and those who did not. Nevertheless, the doctor should check your teen's height and weight regularly. In addition, all children and teens need a nutritious, balanced diet to support growth and development. Making sure your teen eats a well-rounded diet is particularly important if his or her appetite has been decreased as a side effect of the medication.

- Tics. Occasionally, stimulant use may unmask previously unseen tics in teens with an underlying disposition to them. The tics themselves are not harmful. They don't necessarily warrant stopping the medication unless they're bothersome to your teen or your family. If you're concerned, discuss it with your child's doctor.

- Skin color changes. Some users of the methylphenidate patch have developed permanent loss of skin color after repeated exposure to chemical compounds in the patch. The FDA advises watching for new areas of lighter skin, usually (but not always) located around the site where the patch is applied. If your teen has any signs of changing skin color, tell the doctor right away. Although this problem isn't physically harmful, it can be emotionally upsetting for some teens.

Do Fatty Acid Supplements Help?

There's mounting evidence that certain fatty acids might help ease ADHD symptoms in children and adolescents. Eicosapentaenoic acid (EPA), a fatty acid found in fish oil, seems to be mildly effective at reducing ADHD symptoms, especially inattention.

Research results look even more promising when EPA is combined with two other fatty acids: docosahexaenoic acid (DHA), also found in fish oil, and gamma-linolenic acid (GLA), found in evening primrose oil. This isn't a quick fix, however. In studies to date, it took three to six months for any effects to be felt, and even then the benefits were modest.

Use of fatty acid supplements to help manage ADHD is no substitute for proven treatments, such as medication and behavioral therapy. If you're thinking about giving your teen any type of dietary supplement, discuss it with the doctor first. Some supplements may interact with medications or cause side effects. For example, fish oil supplements have been known to cause belching, indigestion, and diarrhea.

Non-stimulant Medications for ADHD

Stimulants are the first-choice medication for most adolescents with ADHD, but they aren't right for everyone. Some teens find that stimulant medications don't work well for them or cause unacceptable side effects. Other teens have medical conditions that rule out the use of stimulants or make using them risky. And still other teens have a history of abusing drugs, which may prompt doctors and parents to look for medications with less potential for abuse or to suspend the use of medication for a while.

In all these scenarios, it's good to know that there are alternatives available. In general, non-stimulant medications aren't quite as effective as stimulants for reducing the symptoms of ADHD. But they do help to some extent, and that makes them a good backup plan for situations in which stimulant medications can't be used or have been tried without success.

Types of Non-stimulants

Two types of non-stimulant medications have been FDA approved for treating ADHD.

NOREPINEPHRINE REUPTAKE INHIBITOR
- Atomoxetine (Strattera)

ALPHA$_2$-ADRENERGIC AGONISTS
- Clonidine, extended release (Kapvay)
- Guanfacine, extended release (Intuniv)

These medications affect the brain differently than stimulants. Atomoxetine increases the amount of norepinephrine available for use by the brain. This may improve attentiveness and decrease hyperactivity and impulsivity. Unlike stimulants, however, atomoxetine doesn't have a direct impact on dopamine—a brain chemical that not only affects attention and movement but also activates the brain's pleasure center. Consequently, atomoxetine does not have the potential to be abused.

Clonidine and guanfacine affect brain cells by activating certain *receptors*—molecules that pick up specific chemical signals, leading to a particular response in the cells. The receptors activated by clonidine and guanfacine are located in the pre-frontal cortex, which may enhance functioning in this key area of the brain that is involved in organization, planning, and self-control.

All of the non-stimulant medications can be used alone to treat ADHD. Clonidine and guanfacine have also been FDA approved for use as an *adjunctive therapy*—a treatment that's added to another treatment to boost its effects. Some teens with ADHD who take stimulants find that their symptoms decrease a little, but not enough. Adding clonidine or guan-facine to the stimulant may lead to greater improvement than either medication alone.

Atomoxetine hasn't been specifically approved for use as an adjunctive therapy, but doctors may still prescribe it that way. Studies suggest that the combination of atomoxetine plus a stimulant may be helpful for some people with ADHD, but more research is needed.

Atomoxetine: Pros and Cons

Atomoxetine, taken once or twice daily, helps reduce inatten-tion, hyperactivity, and impulsivity in children and adoles-cents. And that, in turn, may improve how well they function in their everyday lives.

Often, atomoxetine is prescribed for kids who have co-occurring conditions or experience bothersome side effects when taking stimulants. For example, about one-fourth of children and adolescents with ADHD have an anxiety dis-order, and stimulants sometimes make the anxiety worse. Atomoxetine doesn't have this side effect. In fact, research sug-gests that it may actually lessen anxiety.

Similarly, children and teens with ADHD are more likely than those without ADHD to have tics. Most of the time, stimulant medications don't make the tics worse. Occasionally, however, use of stimulants may trigger or slightly worsen tics in young people. In these cases, collaboration with your child's doctor is needed. It may be possible to use another stimulant. But for some teens, switching to a non-stimulant such as atomoxetine may be indicated.

Another advantage of atomoxetine is that it doesn't have potential for abuse. That could be an important consideration for teens with a history of either abusing drugs themselves or selling or giving away stimulant medications.

On the downside, when people first begin treatment with atomoxetine, it may take a couple of weeks for any signs of improvement to appear. It typically takes 4 to 12 weeks—and occasionally longer—for the full benefits to be seen. You and your teen need to give the medication a chance to work, even if it doesn't seem to be helping right away.

Unlike stimulants, atomoxetine must be taken every day. Your teen can't take it only on school days but not on the weekends, for example.

Atomoxetine: Side Effects and Safety Issues

Atomoxetine should always be taken immediately after eating a meal because nausea, vomiting, or abdominal pain are likely if the medication is taken on an empty stomach. Other common side effects of atomoxetine in children and teens include decreased appetite, dizziness, tiredness, and mood swings. As with any medication, let the doctor know about side effects that are bothersome or persistent. In most cases, the side effects can be managed.

Less commonly, more serious side effects may occur. Like stimulants, atomoxetine may potentially contribute to heart health risks, new mental health problems, and growth delays.

(See the previous section Stimulants: Side Effects and Safety Issues for more details.) In addition, discuss the following safety concerns with your child's doctor:

- Suicidal thinking. Research in more than 2,200 children and teens with ADHD suggests that atomoxetine may slightly increase the risk for suicidal thoughts and behavior, although there were no actual suicides among study participants. The risk of having suicidal thoughts may be highest soon after starting atomoxetine or during dosage adjustments. Watch for sudden changes in your teen's mood and behavior. Be alert for new or severe symptoms such as anxiety, agitation, panic attacks, trouble sleeping, irritability, hostility, aggressiveness, impulsivity, restlessness, mania, depression, or thoughts of suicide. Call the doctor right away if these problems occur. Let the doctor know if your teen has a history of bipolar disorder or suicidal thoughts or behavior.

- Liver problems. There have been rare reports of severe liver damage in people taking atomoxetine. If your teen develops unusual itching, pain in the right upper belly, dark urine, unexplained flu-like symptoms, or yellowish skin or eyes, contact the doctor immediately.

Clonidine ER and Guanfacine ER: Pros and Cons

Clonidine and guanfacine belong to a group of medications that have long been used to treat high blood pressure. Researchers discovered that extended-release (ER) versions of these drugs also helped improve attentiveness and decrease hyperactivity and impulsivity. Eventually, these drugs became an approved class of ADHD medications. Clonidine ER is taken twice a day to treat ADHD, and guanfacine ER is taken once a day.

Some of the initial studies of these medications raised questions about their benefit for adolescents with ADHD. However, more recent research using a higher dose of medication than the original studies suggests that they may be beneficial.

Unlike stimulants, these medications don't have potential for abuse. In some cases, they're taken in place of a stimulant. This may be a good option for teens who have a history of abusing drugs or alcohol or of selling or sharing stimulant medication.

In other cases, these medications may be taken in addition to a stimulant to boost the overall treatment effect. When this combination of drugs is used, the amount of stimulant medication required to manage ADHD can sometimes be reduced.

Clonidine ER and guanfacine ER should be taken as directed every day. Because this type of medication affects blood pressure and heart rate, you can't start and stop it abruptly the way you can a stimulant. To prevent a sudden drop in blood pressure or heart rate when treatment first begins, the medication is started at a low dose and then gradually increased.

It takes a while for these drugs to build up in your teen's system, so don't expect to see results overnight. The first signs of improvement may take one to two weeks to show up, and the full benefits typically take about five weeks to kick in. It's important for your teen to stick with the prescribed medication plan throughout these early weeks, even if the benefits aren't readily apparent yet.

If you and your teen think it might be time to stop clonidine ER or guanfacine ER, discuss this step with the doctor. Halting the medication suddenly may lead to a rapid rise in blood pressure and heart rate, headache, dizziness, nervousness, and tightness in the chest. To prevent such withdrawal symptoms, your teen's doctor needs to give instructions for tapering off the dose gradually.

Clonidine ER and Guanfacine ER: Side Effects and Safety Issues

Common side effects of clonidine ER and guanfacine ER include sleepiness, tiredness, and dizziness. Because drowsiness behind the wheel is so dangerous, your teen should watch out for sleepiness when first starting the medication or after the dose has been adjusted. If the medication makes your teen drowsy when driving or attending school, then it's probably not the best choice for your child. Also, if your teen drinks alcohol while taking one of these drugs, that could make such side effects worse.

Another common side effect of these medications is a slight lowering of blood pressure or heart rate. To make sure these numbers don't dip too low, the doctor should check your teen's blood pressure and heart rate regularly during treatment.

These are some other safety issues to discuss with your child's doctor:

- Fainting. Becoming dehydrated or overheated while taking clonidine ER or guanfacine ER may lead to fainting. Remind your teen to drink plenty of fluids, especially during vigorous physical activity and in hot weather.
- Heart problems. Rarely, these drugs may cause more severe cardiovascular effects, including problems with electrical signaling inside the heart. Contact the doctor right away if your teen experiences a fast or slow heart rate, pounding heartbeats, chest tightness, numbness or tingling, or if your teen feels like passing out.

Choosing a Treatment Strategy

When making decisions about medication for your adolescent with ADHD, it's important to look at both sides of the issue. On the one hand, there are risks and side effects associated with all medications, including those used to treat ADHD. On the other hand, there are very real risks associated with letting ADHD spiral out of control.

ADHD that isn't well managed may interfere with many aspects of your teen's life. Relationships with family and friends may be strained. Grades may plummet as teachers and classes become more demanding. For teens who have jobs, performance at work may be affected. As the problems pile up, the risk rises for disruptive behavior, substance abuse, risky sexual behavior, juvenile delinquency, and dropping out of school.

You and your teen, working together with a doctor you trust, need to make an informed, balanced decision about what's best for your child. For adolescents as a group, the American Academy of Pediatrics (AAP) offers this general recommendation in its treatment guideline: "Given the risks of untreated ADHD, the benefits outweigh the risks." The AAP rates the scientific evidence for this recommendation as "strong."

If you, your teen, and your teen's doctor agree to explore the medication route, the next step is finding a drug that works well for your child. To briefly recap: Typically, the first medication that's prescribed is a stimulant. That's because, as a group, stimulants generally lead to a larger positive effect than that of non-stimulants. The doctor then will work to find the right medicine and dose to get the most benefit with the fewest adverse effects. This adjustment process is more likely to be successful when the teen's response to the medication is closely monitored.

If the initial medication fails to produce enough improvement or causes unacceptable side effects, the doctor may switch to either a different type of stimulant or a non-stimulant. At times, both a stimulant and a non-stimulant may be combined.

Medication Plus Behavioral Therapy

Adding behavioral approaches to the mix may enhance the effectiveness of ADHD treatment even more. The Multimodal Treatment of ADHD (MTA) study, sponsored by the National Institute of Mental Health, is the only study that has carefully examined the long-term effectiveness of medication, behavioral therapy, or both.

When the MTA began, nearly 600 children with ADHD, ages seven to nine, were randomly assigned to one of four groups: intensive medication management, intensive behavioral therapy, both, or neither. (The last group still received routine care by their usual providers.) Intensive medication management involved careful adjustment of the dose followed by monthly doctor visits. Intensive behavioral therapy included child, parent, and school components.

The study lasted for 14 months. By the end, ADHD symptoms had eased in all four groups. However, the largest reductions in ADHD symptoms were seen in the intensive medication and combined treatment groups. Moreover, the greatest improvements in critical areas of functioning—including academic performance, interpersonal relationships, and parent–child relationships—were found among children who received behavioral therapy along with medication.

Six to eight years later, when the children were teens, the researchers checked in to see how they were faring. By this point, years since the intensive treatment had ended, differences among the groups had vanished. The study clearly highlights the need for ongoing treatment for youth with ADHD, which may often require intensive treatment during challenging periods of development.

Teaming Up with Your Teen's Doctor

If your teen with ADHD isn't currently on medication but the two of you are open to this option, your first stop should be your teen's primary care doctor. (In this book, we use the term *doctor* for simplicity's sake. However, primary care providers aren't always physicians. In many states, nurse practitioners and physician assistants may fill this role and prescribe ADHD medication. If your teen's primary care doctor doesn't feel particularly knowledgeable about and comfortable with ADHD medication, ask if there's another doctor in the practice who does.

Occasionally, your teen's primary care doctor might make a referral to a specialist. This could be a child and adolescent psychiatrist or pediatric neurologist. Or it could be a developmental-behavioral pediatrician—a pediatrician who focuses on the assessment and treatment of children and adolescents with developmental, learning, and behavioral problems.

If the doctor prescribes ADHD medication, make sure you know how to use it properly. These are some questions you may want to ask the doctor:

- How much medication should my child take, and when?
- Should my child take the medication every day or just on school days?
- Should my child take it before, with, or between meals?
- What should I do if my child forgets a dose?

- How long will it take for the medication to begin working?
- How can I tell if the medication is working the way it should?
- What are the common side effects, and what should I do if they occur?
- What are the rarer but serious side effects, and what should I do if they occur?
- How should this medication be stored?

Remember that obtaining a prescription for your teen is only the beginning. While taking medication, your teen will need regular doctor's appointments to monitor how things are going. When your teen first starts a new medication, these appointments will generally be spaced close together, about a month apart. Once your teen has settled into a stable medication routine, the interval between in-office visits may lengthen to three, four, or more months apart. If concerns come up between visits, be sure to contact the doctor's office.

Filling the Prescription

Some ADHD medications are pricey, and having health insurance that covers your teen doesn't always make them affordable. The amount you end up paying varies depending on:

- Your insurance plan's deductible, copay, and coinsurance
- Your insurance plan's drug list, which may classify a particular medication as a generic, preferred brand, non-preferred brand, or specialty drug
- Whether you have the prescription filled at a pharmacy in your plan's network

If you have trouble affording your teen's prescription, talk with the doctor who prescribed it. In some cases, there might be a less expensive, generic version of the drug that works just as well for your teen.

In other cases, help might be available from a prescription assistance program. Most states and many pharmaceutical companies offer such programs, which provide free or low-cost medications to qualifying individuals. Your doctor or pharmacist may be able to point you toward a program. Or you can visit the websites of the Partnership for Prescription Assistance (pparx.org) and the Patient Assistance Program Center (rxassist. org) to search for programs that your family may qualify for.

Under federal law, stimulant medications are classified as Schedule II controlled substances with the potential for abuse. As such, stimulants are subject to special requirements that don't apply to most prescriptions. For example, some states and many insurance companies limit the amount of stimulant medication that may be dispensed at one time to a 30-day supply.

Schedule II prescriptions can't be refilled. Your teen's doctor must issue a new prescription each time. You and the doctor's office need to work together to ensure that your teen doesn't run out of medication in special circumstances, such as when your child is out of town for an extended time.

When Your Teen Rejects Medication

Now that your child is an adolescent, he or she needs to be part of the discussion about the benefits and risks of ADHD medication. Although *you* may agree to drug treatment for your child, the doctor should ask for your teen's assent as well. At times, that could be a stumbling block—and even if your teen agrees in the doctor's office, it could be a different story once you get home. In some cases, teens who have been taking medication successfully for years suddenly decide they don't want to take it any longer.

In the case of one teenager named Sofia, she had been doing well on medication since fourth grade. During her senior year in high school, however, she stopped taking it. "She thinks the medication makes her more serious and focused and tuned in," says her mother. "But that's not who she wants to be. She's very social, and she just likes being around friends and doing fun things. She thinks she's more fun and free and silly when she's off her medication."

For teens such as Sofia, the attention-harnessing power of ADHD medication may actually be seen as a drawback. These teens view themselves as less spontaneous and funny when they're on the medication. At an age when winning the attention and approval of friends can seem like the most important thing in the world, some teens may believe that ADHD medication cramps their style.

Other teens may believe that they don't need medication any more because their ADHD symptoms have been under control for a while. And still others may simply be tired of taking a daily pill. Although the rationale varies, the result is often the same: not taking medication, which means missing out on its benefits.

What You Can Do

There might come a time when you and your teen's doctor believe that ADHD medication is still a good idea, but your teen has a different opinion. If this happens, it can be very frustrating, but try to respond with patience. Becoming angry just draws the battle lines, making it more likely that your teen will become firmly entrenched on the other side.

Instead, try to understand your teen's point of view. Start a conversation about your teen's concerns, and really listen to what your child has to say. You may think your teen's views are misguided, but be respectful. Dismissing the concerns as silly or immature is a surefire way to bring the conversation to a screeching halt.

When it's your turn to talk, hopefully your teen will be just as open to listening to and respecting your point of view. You have a better chance of being heard if you've already established a close relationship based on strong communication and negotiation skills. You'll find pointers on how to do that in the next chapter.

Share what you've learned about ADHD medication with your teen. This information may be better received if you present it in the FYI manner you would use with a friend, rather than couching it as a command. You can steer your teen toward reliable resources for further information. And you can encourage your teen to discuss any concerns at the next doctor's appointment. Frequently, a teen will be more accepting of a medication when speaking with the doctor.

It may also be helpful to open a dialogue about the life goals that are most important to your teen right now, whether that means excelling at a sport, getting into a first-choice college, or pursuing a career ambition. Talk about shorter-term objectives that need to be achieved to meet the long-term goals, such as getting A's and B's on tests to be in a position to get accepted by desired colleges. In addition, discuss strategies for achieving objectives and challenges to getting there. In the context of this discussion, your teen can consider how having ADHD might affect attaining his or her goals. Given a chance to think things through and a major voice in the decision, your teen may reach the conclusion that taking medication is the right choice.

Ultimately, however, you can't force your teen to take medication. If he or she remains adamantly opposed, the two of you will need to focus even more effort on managing ADHD through non-drug methods. You might say to your teen: "I understand your concerns, and I appreciate the fact that you've been really open about discussing them. I thought you were great at the doctor's visit, too. You handled the conversation with the doctor very maturely. It's your right to decide whether or not to take medicine. But if you decide not to take medicine, it's going to be vital for us to have a really strong behavioral plan."

Then be prepared to follow through if your teen still chooses the medication-free path. That may mean developing a more comprehensive behavioral contract than would otherwise be necessary. It may also require intensive behavioral management strategies not only at home but also in conjunction with the school. You'll need to work closely with school personnel, and you might also want to seek guidance from a behavioral therapist.

Heading Off Drug Abuse and Diversion

Many parents have their own concerns about ADHD medication, and worries related to drug abuse are often at the top of the list. Some parents fear that, if their children take medication for years, the kids will grow up believing there's nothing wrong with misusing their prescription or abusing other drugs.

Fortunately, that fear hasn't been borne out by experience. It's true that adolescents with ADHD have an increased risk of abusing drugs. But when researchers have compared children with ADHD who either took or did not take stimulants, they've found no difference in the risk of later substance abuse.

In other words, stimulant medication seems to neither increase nor decrease the risk directly.

There may even be an indirect protective effect, however. When teens with ADHD abuse drugs, it's often part of a larger pattern of rule breaking and disruptive behavior. Those who go on to develop full-fledged ODD or conduct disorder are at particularly high risk for substance abuse problems. Well-treated ADHD actually helps prevent the emergence of these conditions. And best-practice treatment for ADHD generally includes both well-monitored drug therapy and behavioral home and school interventions.

What if you suspect that your teen with ADHD may already be abusing drugs or alcohol? It's vital to share this information with the treatment team. If a professional assessment shows that your teen likely does have a drug or alcohol problem, this needs to be addressed sooner rather than later. Generally speaking, your teen's doctor will want to see progress toward managing the substance abuse problem before starting or continuing medication to treat ADHD.

Once progress is being made on the substance abuse front, the doctor will take your child's drug and alcohol history into account when choosing an ADHD medication. The doctor might prescribe a non-stimulant. Or the doctor might prescribe one of the stimulants that are formulated in a way that makes them harder to abuse. These stimulants include Daytrana (methylphenidate patch), Vyvanse (lisdexamfetamine), and Concerta (methylphenidate).

Preventing Stimulant Abuse

Whether or not your teen has a history of other types of substance abuse, it's important to educate your child about the risks of abusing stimulant medication. In order to do that, you need to understand the risks yourself. One excellent resource for the two of you to explore together is NIDA for Teens (teens.drugabuse.gov), run by the National Institute on Drug Abuse.

When taken as prescribed to treat ADHD, stimulant medications don't produce a high. However, they can be abused by taking them in a greater quantity or a different manner than the doctor intended. People who abuse stimulants sometimes crush the pills and then snort the powder, or they may mix it with water and inject it.

Stimulants used as directed for ADHD lead to a slow, steady rise in dopamine levels—an increase that mimics the way dopamine is normally released by the brain. But stimulants that are taken in excessive amounts or by alternate routes can lead to an unnatural surge in dopamine, producing a high feeling and potentially addiction.

As with other abused drugs, getting high on stimulants can lead to terrible judgment and dangerous behavior. People who repeatedly abuse stimulants may also become hostile and paranoid. In addition, regular stimulant abusers may experience such severe loss of appetite that they develop malnutrition and its consequences. At high doses, stimulants can cause life-threatening cardiovascular problems, including stroke.

Pass along the facts. And when you do, remember: Your words of warning are more likely to have the desired effect on your teen when you've already established a strong relationship and an open line of communication.

Preventing Medication Sharing

Even teens who would never think of abusing their stimulant medication themselves may feel pressured to sell it to others or share it with friends. Health care and law enforcement professionals use the term *drug diversion* for this practice of redirecting a prescribed medication into an unlawful, non-prescribed use.

Drug diversion is a crime, which could have serious legal repercussions for anyone who sells or gives away stimulant medication. It's also a reckless act, which isn't doing the person on the receiving end any favors. If a stimulant is used improperly, it can be harmful. And even if the stimulant is taken in the usual way, it might be unsafe when used by someone other than the person for whom it was prescribed. Doctors screen patients for medical conditions that increase the risks of taking a particular medication. But a teen passing along a few pills to a classmate has no way of knowing about any such underlying medical risks.

Many parents are shocked to discover how widespread the problem is. Stimulant medications are abused recreationally. And because they may greatly increase wakefulness and decrease appetite in those without ADHD, they're also abused by teens who want to lose weight or stay up all night cramming for a test. It's common for students with ADHD prescriptions to be approached about selling or giving away their medication as early as middle school. The problem only gets worse in high school and college.

Once again, honest communication between you and your teen is paramount. Discuss the serious consequences of drug diversion. Encourage your teen to tell you if he or she has ever felt bullied or coerced into sharing medication. Beyond that, your teen benefits when other trusted adults— such as an aunts, uncles, coaches, teachers, and youth group leaders—reinforce this important message and offer their support.

Are Stimulants Effective Study Aids?

The classmates who approach your teen about selling or giving away prescription stimulants aren't always rebels looking for a thrill. A growing number are serious students seeking a competitive edge.

Many young people believe that taking prescription stimulants will enhance their ability to study and learn. In reality, students with ADHD often do perform better in school when they're taking their prescribed medication. But that's because the medication helps reduce ADHD symptoms—not because it's an IQ-boosting elixir.

When used by students without ADHD, prescription stimulants can keep people awake for long periods. That might seem helpful for those trying to pull an all-nighter before a big test, but it turns out to be counterproductive. Research has shown that taking stimulants doesn't boost learning. In fact, high school and college students who abuse stimulants generally have lower grade point averages than those who don't.

Monitoring Medication Use

Parental supervision is another key to preventing stimulant abuse and diversion. An adolescent may gradually assume more responsibility for taking his or her own medication. But you should still keep a watchful eye on how things are going.

Try to spend some time with your teen every morning, even if it's just a couple of minutes over breakfast. This gives you a chance to observe your teen actually taking the medication. A predictable routine that links taking medication to a daily activity, such as eating breakfast, also helps your teen remember the medicine every day.

Check the medicine bottle on a regular basis to make sure it contains the right amount of medication. If the bottle goes from full to half-empty in a couple of days, you know there's a problem that needs to be addressed. Store the medication in a secure place where siblings and visiting friends can't take it accidentally or on purpose.

ADHD Treatment: Putting It All Together

Up to this point, we've focused on the role of your teen's doctor. Yet it bears repeating that managing ADHD is a team sport, not an individual event. The core positions on the team include:

- Family: you, your partner (or anyone else who shares parenting duties), your teen
- Health care: your teen's doctor, your teen's therapist
- School: your teen's teachers, the school psychologist, other school personnel

Ideally, these three groups should coordinate their efforts seamlessly. There may also be supporting players, such as community agencies and after-school programs. In a perfect world, they should be fully integrated into the treatment plan as well.

In the real world, the pieces of your teen's treatment may not fall into place quite this neatly. You can help unify the process by making sure everyone is working toward the same goals. These goals should take into account your and your teen's preferences and priorities for treatment.

Don't be afraid to speak up. Don't hesitate to ask questions. And don't be surprised if this year's goals are a little different from those of the year before.

Key Points

- Your teen's ADHD symptoms may no longer respond to the same medication regimen that worked well before. A change in medication, dose, or dosage schedule may be required.

- Stimulants are the best studied and most effective class of ADHD medication. They're also the most commonly prescribed.
- Common side effects of stimulant medications include headaches, stomach aches, decreased appetite, and sleep problems.
- Non-stimulant medications are available for situations in which stimulants can't be used or have been tried without success.
- About 20% to 30% of young people with ADHD don't respond to the first stimulant that's prescribed. Work with your teen's doctor to find the best medication regimen for your teen.

Learn More

For the latest information about medications for ADHD, go to the FDA website (fda.gov) and search for "ADHD" or a specific medication name.

Chapter Five

Your Teen at Home: Building Strong Bonds and Positive Behavior Patterns

Many factors play a role in successful child develop-ment, but none is more important than a strong, loving parent–child relationship. That's true for babies, preschoolers, and school-aged kids. And it's equally true for adolescents.

Yet, by the time you reach your child's teenage years, it's understandable if you're starting to feel a little tired. Raising any child is a big job, and raising a child with ADHD entails additional challenges. In some families, relationships break under the added strain.

Fortunately, there are steps you can take to keep that from happening. In this chapter, you'll find specific, evidence-based strategies for maintaining a strong parent–child relationship or rebuilding a shaky one. These strategies boil down to seven big ideas:

- Make time for one-on-one activities.
- Listen carefully to your teen.
- Be a firm, but warm and loving parent.
- Show affection in meaningful ways.
- Provide appropriate rules and supervision.

- Foster communication and problem-solving.
- Affirm successes and limit criticism.

Staying Involved in Your Teen's Life

When your child was younger, spending time together was not only a pleasure but also a necessity. You can't let a four-year-old wander unsupervised through the mall, and you can't allow an eight-year-old to drive to a friend's house. Now that your child is older and more independent, however, you may wonder if your presence is still required.

The answer is yes, absolutely. Just spending time with your teen is one of the most powerful ways of showing how much you care. Engage in some one-on-one activities that genuinely interest your child. Depending on your teen, that might mean shopping for clothes, cooking a fancy meal, rebuilding a car engine, or going to a ball game.

Beyond that, show up for school and community events to support your teen. If your child is playing in a sports tournament or singing in a school musical, make every effort to attend. Realistically, there will likely be times when you have work or family conflicts, and you can't be in two places at once. But know that each time you *do* show up, your teen notices.

Even when you can't be there in person, know what's going on in your teen's life. Some parents question whether their involvement really continues to matter as kids get older. In fact, there's strong evidence that parents still have a huge impact.

For instance, one study looked at whether being diagnosed with ADHD in childhood predicted alcohol use by age 17. When parents had less knowledge of their teens' whereabouts, activities, and friends, alcohol use was more frequent in teens with ADHD than in those without the condition. But when parents knew more about their teens' lives, the association between ADHD and alcohol use decreased. This is just one of many examples of the difference that parents can make by staying actively involved.

Tony's Story

Another way to reaffirm your relationship with your child is by shining a light on positive behavior. At times, however, finding the bright spots can take some extra effort.

In Nikki's case, she struggled to stay positive after her son with ADHD had trouble making the transition to college. "He had to withdraw from an entire semester at a private university because he messed up," she recalls. "That's all money down the drain."

Nikki's son, Tony, had been diagnosed with behavioral problems and Tourette syndrome at a young age. By third grade, he was diagnosed with ADHD, and his younger brother soon followed suit. A dedicated and determined mom, Nikki poured a lot of herself into learning about ADHD and advocating for her boys with the school. Eventually, she became known around the community as a bulwark of support for other parents in similar situations.

Then, just when it seemed like Nikki might have it all figured out, Tony floundered during spring semester at college. The unexpected setback was deeply discouraging for both mother and son. "I was in a really bad place," Nikki says. "The only way I got out of it was by creating an electronic notebook. Every day, I wrote down five things I noticed that he was doing right. Then I would email the list to him."

Nikki and Tony kept up this routine throughout the summer. "I think it helped Tony stand a little taller every day," Nikki says. "But the journal also had a really profound impact on me. Thinking about the good things took away the weight of the fear and the negativity. By the time we got to September, we were both re-energized."

Ryan's Story

Of course, not all families communicate so well. In Ryan's family, for instance, what were once little cracks in relationships have recently grown into chasms.

Twenty-year-old Ryan, a college student, lives at home with his parents and two younger siblings. Since high school, he and his dad have clashed over Ryan's drug use, poor grades, and "bad attitude." "Ryan has big issues with his father," says his mom, Beth. "At this point, they don't speak anymore even though we're all under the same roof."

Before things got this far, Beth tried holding family meetings, where she, her husband, and her son could talk about issues. "Ryan would say something. But then my husband would say something reacting to it that wasn't really understanding what Ryan was trying to say, so I would try to translate," says Beth. "But then Ryan would say something back, and he wouldn't really understand what my husband meant either, so I would try to translate that, too."

The family meetings never seemed to resolve anything. "It was like Ryan and his father were on two different planes," Beth says. "And I would be caught in the middle all the time, which was a stumbling block for me."

Eventually, Beth stopped trying to play mediator and began excluding her husband from the conversation. "I used to run everything past my husband, but he was constantly so hard on Ryan," says Beth. "After a while, I just took my husband out of the equation so I could start moving forward with Ryan. Basically, now I just let my husband know what I'm doing but I've taken him out of the decision-making."

The rifts within Ryan's family have been painful for everyone. Yet even when tensions run this high, it's not too late to bridge divides and mend fractured relationships. One of the first steps is rethinking your approach to parenting now that your child is getting older.

Being an Authoritative (Not Authoritarian) Parent

Parenting is a balancing act. On the one hand, parents want to be their children's allies. On the other hand, they need to be in charge and willing to enforce rules. Research shows that teens thrive when parents find a happy medium between too permissive and too controlling.

Striking that balance can be tricky, however, especially with a teen who has ADHD. By their children's teen years, parents have been grappling with the challenges of ADHD for years, and many are dealing with defiant or disruptive behavior as well. Some react by giving up, while others clamp down so hard that they become dictatorial. Neither of these parenting extremes is productive. In fact, they may promote irresponsible or rebellious behavior and inflame tensions at home.

These are some signs that parenting may have veered off course:

- Too permissive. Overly lenient parents go along with whatever their teens want. They either don't set rules or they don't enforce the rules consistently. Some parents also stop providing supervision. They don't know where their teens are or what their teens are doing. That's particularly dangerous, because teens who engage in a lot of unsupervised activity outside the home are more likely to make risky choices.

- Too controlling. Overly strict parents try to control every aspect of their teens' lives. They don't allow their teens an appropriate amount of freedom and independence. When an overly controlling style is combined with lots of affection, it can feel smothering and intrusive. When it's combined with a low degree of affection, it can come across as authoritarian and domineering. Either way, when parents act too controlling, teens often respond by becoming stubborn and oppositional. It's a vicious cycle that can fuel family conflict and seriously erode the parent–child relationship.

Balancing Affection and Control

Psychologist Diana Baumrind has conducted some of the seminal research on this subject. She uses the term *authoritative parenting* to describe a child-rearing style that falls in the sweet spot between the two extremes. Authoritative parents exhibit these qualities:

HIGH IN AFFECTION
- Express affection without being smothering
- Affirm and genuinely like their children

MODERATELY HIGH IN CONTROL
- Set appropriate rules and enforce them effectively
- Provide close supervision throughout adolescence

Showing Affection and Giving Affirmation

Adolescents thrive when parents are warm and affectionate. Yet they may want their parents to back off on overt displays of affection, especially in public. You might have picked up on that. Chances are, the same child who happily walked into kindergarten hand-in-hand with you wouldn't want to walk into ninth grade with you anywhere in sight.

That doesn't mean your child wants you to pull away completely, however. Look for ways of showing affection that are accepted and appreciated. For example, a teen who would rather you didn't shout out "Love you!" in front of a group of teammates may appreciate hearing those words at home every morning before leaving for school.

Another way to show your affection is by catching your teen being good and commending examples of responsibility, cooperation, and thoughtfulness. In families where people are quick to affirm and appreciate each other, there tends to be less conflict. And when you do need to correct your teen's behavior, your words may carry more weight. Big punishments, such as grounding, may be needed less frequently.

Setting and Enforcing House Rules

When it comes to general house rules, adolescents do best when parents are firm but fair. Establish clear, consistent expectations for your teen's behavior. These are some general guidelines rooted in proven behavioral principles:

- Limit the number of house rules so that you and your teen can stay focused on the most important ones.
- Be sure your teen knows exactly what you expect and what the consequences of breaking the rules will be.
- Monitor your teen's behavior closely so you'll know whether your teen is actually following the rules.
- Be quick to notice and acknowledge when your teen has complied with the rules.

- Make the punishment fit the "crime" when there's an infraction. Ideally, it should be a logical consequence.
- Avoid harsh or frequent punishment. It's ineffective and may increase defiance and rule breaking.

As an example, consider your teen's curfew. Ensuring that your teen gets home safely every day certainly qualifies as important enough to warrant having a rule. Make sure your teen knows exactly what time curfew is for weeknights and weekends. Then follow up by monitoring when your teen actually gets home.

If your teen misses the curfew, a logical consequence might be to forfeit time the next day. So a teen who gets in 20 minutes late on Friday night might be required to come home 20 minutes early on Saturday night. For a typical adolescent, that's likely to be a bigger deal than it would be for an adult, because spending as much time as possible with friends is such a high priority. For an impulsive teen with ADHD, the significance may be further magnified by a distorted sense of time, which can make 20 minutes feel much longer than it really is.

In the case of a more serious curfew violation, you might have a more serious consequence, such as grounding for all of Saturday. However, grounding your teen for a whole week is unlikely to be effective. Your teen doesn't get a chance to practice what he or she has learned about the importance of coming home on time. You lose leverage, because there are fewer privileges to take away if your teen breaks another rule during the grounding period. And you risk losing credibility, too, if you gradually slack off on enforcing the punishment.

Ultimately, if grounding drags on for too long, you and your teen may lose sight of the infraction that originally prompted it. But you'll still be acutely aware of the ongoing friction that exists well after the punishment is applied. Teens with ADHD are already at higher risk for oppositional behavior and conduct problems, and ratcheting up the conflict may only make things worse.

Providing Supervision and Promoting Independence

Teens whose parents provide close supervision are less likely to make risky choices that end up hurting themselves or others. A reasonable level of supervision for adolescents means:

- You know where your teen is throughout the day.
- You can verify your teen's whereabouts at any time.
- When your teen is away from home, you have a good idea of what your teen is doing and who else is there.

Of course, the extent to which you keep tabs on your child's whereabouts, activities, and friends will naturally evolve as your child becomes more mature. For example, if a middle-schooler asks to spend the afternoon at a new friend's house, you might insist on not only meeting the friend but also speaking with the friend's parents. In addition, you may drop off and pick up your child, and you may expect that your child and the friend will stay at the house unless they have permission to go elsewhere.

As your child matures and exhibits more responsibility, it's appropriate and expected to gradually start loosening the reins. Just keep in mind that teens with ADHD often lag behind their peers developmentally. You can't assume that your 16-year-old is ready for the same level of responsibility as the 16-year-old down the block.

Instead, you need to individualize decisions about how much freedom your child is—and is not—mature enough to handle. That can be a tricky call at times. When you're feeling unsure about what to do, try asking for input from relatives and friends who know your child well and whose judgment you trust. Talking things through with other parents in an ADHD support group may help you reach a decision as well. If you're still stuck, or if you and your partner disagree about when it's time to let go, a mental health professional may be able to help.

Should Your Teen Be on a Special Diet?

An elimination diet is used to identify specific foods (such as sugar) or food additives (such as artificial colorings) that may be causing symptoms in an individual. Such diets have been touted for managing ADHD since the 1970s. Yet despite this long history, they remain controversial.

In this approach, one or more foods are removed from a person's diet for a few weeks to see whether symptoms improve. Then the foods are reintroduced one at a time to see whether the symptoms return. If a food does indeed seem to be making someone's ADHD symptoms worse, that person might choose to cut it out of his or her diet.

Here's what research shows about the potential connection between diet and ADHD:

- Artificial colorings. In rigorously controlled studies, diets that eliminate food dyes have not been shown to have a large, consistent impact on ADHD symptoms in most children. However, there may be a small subset of kids for whom this approach is beneficial.
- Sugar. Consuming sugar generally has not been shown to cause ADHD in children. However, there is some evidence that it might slightly worsen existing symptoms.

Before you try an elimination diet, check with your teen's doctor to ensure that the dietary restrictions won't have a harmful effect on your child. Keep in mind that your teen needs to eat a nutritious variety of foods. If you're thinking about restricting multiple foods, it may also be advisable to talk with a registered dietitian nutritionist. In addition, make sure that your teen buys into this approach. Otherwise, your teen is unlikely to stick with the diet when you aren't around, and food could become a frequent source of conflict in your relationship.

Bolstering Communication Skills

Good communication lays the foundation for a strong parent–child relationship. When your child has ADHD, communication and negotiation skills are also crucial for collaborative problem-solving. But these skills aren't just helpful at home. They give your teen a leg up at school, at work, and in other relationships.

There are two sides to the communication process—listening and speaking—and both are important. Following are some evidence-based tips on sharpening these skills, both in yourself and in your adolescent with ADHD.

Being a Good Listener

Good listening is the cornerstone of effective communication. Teens with ADHD often have trouble listening attentively and controlling the impulse to interrupt. You can help by spelling out the fundamental rules of conversation: The two of you will take turns speaking, and when it's one person's turn to talk, the other will listen without interrupting. This might seem basic, but it can be challenging for both parents and teens to do.

One helpful listening technique is to periodically restate what your teen has just said, paraphrasing rather than parroting it back word for word. To do that, you need to listen closely to the verbal content of your teen's message. But it also helps to pay attention to the emotional content as well as your teen's intent and values. Then reflect those things back when you restate what you've heard: "You're spending two hours on homework and still not getting it done, and you're feeling frustrated. I know you really want to do well academically, and passing this class is important to you." Doing this demonstrates that you have indeed been listening. It also gives you a chance to double-check that you've understood your teen correctly.

Practice listening many times per day, even for short periods of time, such as when you're riding in the car, sharing a meal, or watching TV together. Allow your teen to control the agenda of the conversation during these times. Often, the best thing you can do is simply to listen to whatever your teen has to say. Then show that you've heard and understood how your teen feels.

What if your teen is the type who just sits there silently? Ask probing questions now and then and avoid framing them in ways that you know from experience will likely lead to one-word answers. ("How was school today?" "OK." "What did you do?" "Nothing.") If your teen still isn't feeling chatty, however, respect that. Resist the temptation to chatter to fill the void and work on feeling comfortable with the silence. You can always try again another time.

Speaking to Be Heard

On the speaking side of the equation, there will undoubtedly be times when you need to express a concern about your teen's behavior. When you're able to do this without coming across as criticizing, berating, or yelling, you're more likely to get a positive reception. At the same time, you're serving as a role model.

Often, the best way to frame a concern is by making an "I" statement: "When you do X, I feel Y." And don't automatically replace the Y with "angry." When you dig a little deeper, angry feelings toward your child are frequently rooted in fear and worry. For example, you might say, "When you don't come home on time, I feel worried about you." This communication helps your teen understand that your reaction is based on deep concern for the safety of your child.

Another useful tactic is pointing out the contrast between what your teen is currently doing and what your teen hopes to achieve in the future. You might frame your statement this way: "I know you're working on X [a goal]. How is Y [a counterproductive behavior] helping you?" For example, imagine that your teen has been worried about flunking math and having to retake it in summer school. You receive a notice from the math teacher saying that your teen hasn't been turning in assignments. You might say, "I know we've been working on bringing up your math grade so you won't have to go to summer school. How is not turning in your assignments helping you?" The idea is to spark a conversation, which may lead to the realization that the behavior isn't helpful at all. And that, in turn, may lead to discussing alternative strategies for reaching the goal.

One trap to avoid is lecturing. When you drone on, your teen is likely to tune out, regardless of what you're saying. Plus, a teen with ADHD may have trouble sustaining attention during a long-winded explanation. If you have something important to say, your teen is more likely to hear it if you're clear, brief, and to the point.

If you've tried brushing up on your speaking and listening skills, and you're still struggling to establish a positive dialogue with your teen, consider seeking advice from a mental health professional. Communication lies at the heart of your relationship. Improving your and your teen's communication skills can have a huge impact on all your interactions.

Collaborating on Solving Problems

ADHD often gives rise to behaviors that can wreak havoc with your home life and family routine. Examples include not getting ready for school on time, leaving belongings scattered around the house, picking on younger siblings, and not completing homework or chores. You and your teen may decide to work together on replacing some of the problem behaviors with more positive ones.

In Chapter Three, you read about the ABCs—antecedents, behavior, and consequences—of behavior change. Learning to apply the ABC approach effectively takes time and effort. Most parents benefit from getting some professional guidance at the outset and during difficult periods. With practice, however, many parents and teens become quite adept at collaborative problem-solving using the ABC framework.

Targeting a Behavior

The first step is to identify the problem on which you want to focus. Then talk with your teen about possible strategies for addressing it. You might start the ball rolling this way: "We've been having a hard time with this issue. Can we discuss what's going on? Maybe we can come up with some ideas about how to improve the situation."

With a younger child, this type of problem-solving is done mainly by you, either alone or in conjunction with other grown-ups, such as teachers and therapists. With an adolescent, however, it's crucial to include your teen in the problem-solving process. A teen who isn't on board with the plan is likely to sabotage it.

Eventually, you'll need to narrow your focus to one or two target behaviors that you and your teen want to change. A good target behavior has these attributes:

- Positive. Try to frame the target as something your teen needs to do more of, rather than less of. For example, let's say the general problem is that your teen isn't walking the dog after school. It's better to state the goal as "walking the dog every afternoon" rather than "being less irresponsible around the house."

- Important. Pick a behavior that's significant enough to justify the work of changing it. Distinguish those behaviors that may be annoying or irritating to you from those that really make a difference to your family. As the saying goes, don't sweat the small stuff.

- Realistic. Select a behavior that you and your teen have a reasonable chance of improving. Particularly when you're starting out, it's helpful to pick a target behavior that's important but not too difficult or controversial.

If you're having trouble picking a target behavior, sit down with your teen. Spend a little time brainstorming about behaviors that are causing problems. At first, just jot down all the ideas that come to mind without evaluating them. Later, go back through the ideas together and create a list of the most important behaviors to target.

Rank these behaviors by how difficult they will be to change. Finally, to give your teen a good shot at success, pick a behavior that is only slightly to moderately difficult to work on. It's critically important for your teen to experience success in the beginning and then to continue experiencing high rates of success as you engage in problem-solving together.

Ultimately, the target behavior should be mutually selected. It's not just your idea. It's something that your teen also agrees would be good to change. Reaching that kind of consensus may be easier if you spell out the benefits for your teen. You might say: "Not only can we address this problem that we've been having, but also you may be able to earn some privileges that you've been wanting. Let's talk about what we can do."

Manipulating Antecedents

The second step in developing an ABC plan is considering the antecedents—things preceding a behavior that influence how likely it is to occur. By manipulating antecedents, you can set your teen up for success. Antecedents vary depending on the individual and the target behavior in question. Here are a few typical examples:

- Physiological antecedents. Hunger and lack of sleep may lead to a bad mood, and that, in turn, may lead to uncooperative behavior. To set the stage for a better attitude, establish a household routine with regular times for eating meals, shutting off electronic devices before bedtime, and going to bed.
- Environmental antecedents. Frequent distractions, such as a TV that's always blaring or a phone that's constantly pinging, may make it harder to pay attention, stay on task, communicate effectively, and engage in healthy family routines, such as mealtimes. To set the stage for improved focus, you might want to establish some house rules for screen time and phone use in your home. For example, you might make a rule that electronic devices and cell phones aren't allowed during meals and for a period of time afterward, which is reserved for reading and homework. You may also want to have a discussion with your teen about when it makes sense—and when it doesn't—to use phones, tablets, and laptops in the bedroom.

When Teens Don't Snooze, They Lose

Lack of enough sleep is a frequent issue for adolescents in general, but it's an especially common problem among teens with ADHD. There are several contributing factors:

- Many teens with ADHD have trouble managing their daily schedules, so they may end up going to bed at unpredictable times or staying up late cramming for tests.
- Teens often use electronic devices late at night, which may prevent them from feeling tired when they should be falling asleep.
- Teens often stay up very late on weekends, which can have a carryover effect on their wake–sleep schedule during the week.
- The stimulant medications used to treat ADHD may also cause sleep disruption as a side effect, although doctors can often minimize this problem by fine-tuning a teen's medication plan.

When adolescents with ADHD don't get enough sleep, it makes it even harder for them to stay focused the next day. But the fallout doesn't end there, according to research by psychologist Stephen Becker and his colleagues. In one study of young adolescents with ADHD, sleep problems were associated with increases in depressive symptoms and oppositional behavior over time. In another study of college students with ADHD, daytime sleepiness was linked to poor school adjustment and the number of D and F grades received, above and beyond what would be expected based on ADHD symptoms alone.

To help your teen get a better night's sleep, establish consistent daily routines and negotiate sensible limits on the use of electronic devices at night. Ideally, homework and studying should be done earlier in the evening rather than waiting until right before bedtime. On weekends, extending the usual bedtime by an hour or so probably won't make that much difference, but pushing it beyond this point could have a negative effect.

Both teens and parents tend to pay less attention to antecedents than to consequences. Yet time put into analyzing and modifying antecedents is time very well spent. It helps stack the deck in favor of successful behavior change.

Managing Consequences to Shape Behavior

The third step in developing an ABC plan is considering the consequences—things following a behavior that influence how likely it is to occur again. By managing consequences consistently and appropriately, you can encourage a desirable behavior or discourage an undesirable one.

Consequences can be divided into four main categories: positive reinforcement, planned ignoring, strategic punishment, and negative reinforcement. When creating a collaborative ABC plan with your teen, focus most of your attention on positive reinforcement—rewards that increase the likelihood that a desirable behavior will be repeated. This fosters a positive climate in your home, which supports optimal learning and successful behavior change.

Your approval and praise are powerfully rewarding, so make a point of noticing and commending good behavior. But bear in mind: Your teen greatly values your attention, so much so that even neutral or negative attention can be rewarding. Make a conscious choice to time more of your attention and engagement to coincide with positive behavior by your teen.

Beyond that, rewards of privileges, money, or material goods can be motivational. You may want to set up a system whereby your teen can earn credits for doing chores, finishing homework, or following rules. The credits can then be redeemed for rewards, based on a menu established in advance. These are some guidelines to keep in mind:

- Pick rewards that are highly meaningful for your teen. Possible examples include outings with friends, use of the family car, allowance money, and material objects (such as nonessential clothes, music downloads, or electronic games). Ask your teen for help in selecting the rewards.

- Establish the exchange menu. List the rewards offered and assign each one a "price"—the number of credits required to obtain it.
- Differentiate between short-term (weekly) and long-term (monthly or longer) rewards. Working toward a big, long-term reward can be a valuable learning experience. But to keep motivation high, make sure there are also smaller rewards along the way.
- Choose a method for tracking the target behavior. For example, your teen might put a checkmark on a chart or send you a text each time a targeted chore is completed.
- Select a method of tracking credits as they're earned. For example, you might keep a running tally on a paper chart, digital log, or white board in the kitchen.

Discouraging Unwanted Behaviors

The ABC plan you hammer out with your teen should focus mainly on increasing desirable behaviors through positive reinforcement. Yet, as a practical matter, you also need to deal with undesirable behaviors as they occur. That's where planned ignoring, strategic punishment, and negative reinforcement come into play.

- Planned ignoring. When deciding how you'll deal with undesirable behaviors, first consider which ones are major problems and which are minor annoyances. Whining and finger-tapping are examples of behaviors you may want to relegate to the latter category. The most effective way to handle such behaviors is often planned ignoring. You don't punish the behaviors, but you don't reward them with attention either. If you feel yourself getting irritated, step away. For example, if your teen's whining is getting to you, pop on your earphones. If fidgeting is fraying your nerves, move to the other room.

- Strategic punishment. Breaking major rules, on the other hand, may call for a punishment, such as losing privileges or forfeiting reward credits. Just remember that punishment is most effective when used sparingly. Aim for *at least* four times more positive reinforcement than punishment. Previously, you read about using grounding as a punishment. As another example, imagine that one of your teen's chores is taking out the trash. It's an essential chore, so you decide that neglecting it qualifies as a punishable offense. If your teen doesn't do it, you offer one prompt. If your teen still doesn't comply, the punishment might be that your teen isn't allowed to leave the house to visit a friend until the trash is handled. Your teen learns that breaking the rule doesn't result in getting out of the chore, but it *does* result in losing a privilege.

A Word About Verbal Correction

When you hear the word *punishment*, you may think about taking away privileges or grounding your teen. But there's another form of punishment that often gets overlooked. Your approval is extremely important to your child. So when you say, "You didn't do this," or "You should have done that," even if you do so gently, it's experienced as an aversive consequence. In other words, it's a mild form of punishment.

Of course, there are times when verbal correction is appropriate. But it's important to be aware of how often and how you use it. Like other forms of punishment, verbal correction is best deployed strategically. Here are some general guidelines:

- Use a calm, emotionally neutral tone of voice.
- State what your teen should do more of, not less of.
- Make your point clearly and concisely.
- Stop once you've made the point; don't belabor it.
- Get in the habit of affirming and praising at least four times more often than correcting your teen.

As soon as you see signs that your teen's behavior is moving in the right direction, be sure to remark on that. Like other rewards and punishments, verbal statements work best when they're heavily weighted toward the positive.

- Negative reinforcement. In contrast, if you just sigh and take out the trash yourself, you're actually providing negative reinforcement. By letting your teen avoid doing something he or she doesn't want to do, you're rewarding that behavior using negative reinforcement. This only makes it more likely that your teen will neglect to take out the trash again. Teens with ADHD are particularly prone to putting off and avoiding tasks that are boring or require sustained attention. Make sure you aren't unintentionally encouraging this kind of behavior with negative reinforcement.

In the short run, getting your teen to do a disliked task may require considerably more effort than simply doing it yourself or leaving it undone. Your teen may try to wear you down by arguing or ignoring you. In the long run, however, you can cut down on future confrontations by calmly but firmly standing your ground.

Teaming Up with Your Teen

It takes a coordinated effort to identify target behaviors and develop strategies for changing them. Strong communication and negotiation skills are vital. If these skills are weak, you and your teen may need to work on bolstering them before going any further.

Once you are ready to discuss an ABC plan, choose a time when you're both rested and getting along well. Find a quiet place to talk where there aren't too many distractions. Then establish some ground rules for your discussion:

- One person speaks at a time.
- The tone remains calm and civil.
- The comments stay on topic.
- Both of you avoid blaming statements.

Ignore occasional, brief lapses in following these rules. After all, no one is a perfect communicator. But if your teen repeatedly violates the rules, end the conversation.

It's always better to stop while things are going smoothly rather than waiting until they're falling apart. So keep your chats brief and don't try to iron out every issue in a single sitting. Some parents even set a timer for five minutes and end the conversation when it goes off. If you're ready to tie things up, you might say: "We're off to a great start. I'll take a couple of notes, and then we can come back and talk some more tomorrow."

Throughout your discussion, be quick to recognize and affirm your teen's contributions. Comment on it when your teen shares ideas, listens to your thoughts, and collaborates with you on finding middle ground.

The eventual aim is to reach a mutual agreement on which behaviors to change and what the consequences of achieving a behavioral goal will be. For example, let's say the agreed-upon goal is for your teen to rinse the dishes and put them in the dishwasher after dinner. You could specify how many reward points your teen earns by doing this. You can also explicitly state that your teen won't receive these points if the chore isn't done in a timely fashion. As a final step, you and your teen may want to formalize your agreement in a written behavioral contract, which both of you sign (see Table 5.1).

Advanced Behavioral Contracts

The Sample Behavioral Contract in Table 5.1 is a typical contract focusing on rewards for compliance. After you and your teen have some experience under your belts, there are times when you might want to also add a punishment for noncompliance. However, the primary focus should still remain on positive reinforcement. As a rule of thumb, a good contract is one that enables your teen to succeed at least 80% of the time.

Table 5.1
Sample Behavioral Contract

Contract is between _____ (Teen) and _____
(Parent) starting on _____ (Date).

Teen agrees to work on the following behaviors:

1. _____ 2. _____

Teen will obtain points for these behaviors. When Teen achieves goals, Parent agrees to provide rewards selected by the teen. Following are the rewards and their point values:

1. _____ Value: _____

2. _____ Value: _____

3. _____ Value: _____

If Teen does not achieve the goals, the rewards are not given. Both parties agree to this contract. If disputes arise, both parties agree to renegotiate in the future.

Signature of Teen: _____ Date: _____

Signature of Parent: _____ Date: _____

Of course, you've been punishing your teen as needed all along. The difference here is that your teen is collaborating with you on choosing the punishment and deciding when it will be used. Specifying the terms of punishment is optional; it's not a necessary component of the behavioral contract. But if you and your teen choose to include punishment in a contract, you should specify:

- What level of the target behavior is needed to receive a reward (such as earning points)
- What level results in failure to earn the reward
- What level leads to punishment and what that punishment will be (such as losing points)

Rebuilding a Damaged Relationship

Reaching the point where you and your teen can sit down and talk calmly about solving problems together is a wonderful objective. But for many families, it takes a while to get there. Years of living with the fallout from ADHD can exact a toll. These are a few of the factors that may damage the parent–child relationship:

- Home issues. Some ADHD symptoms are likely to cause conflict at home—for example, not listening to what parents say, becoming sidetracked during homework, neglecting to do chores, butting into siblings' activities, and not being ready for school in the morning.
- School issues. Students with ADHD may have trouble completing and turning in schoolwork, following the teacher's instructions, and getting along with classmates. Parents may end up in the middle of conflicts between their teens and the school.

- Disruptive behavior. Teens with ADHD are at risk for developing oppositional defiant disorder and conduct disorder—two conditions that cause a lot of additional upheaval.

By the time children with ADHD reach adolescence, the relationship with their parents is frequently frayed. Mending that relationship is a prerequisite for achieving the best results when working with your teen to change problem behaviors.

If you find yourself in this situation, it can be quite stressful. Taking care of yourself allows you to take better care of your teen. Create a support system of family and friends and reach out when the situation at home gets emotionally intense.

If you start thinking that "everything is hopeless" or you're "the worst parent ever," your trusted supporters can be a sounding board for these exaggerated thoughts. They may be able to help you see the situation in a more hopeful, realistic light.

Recognize and respect your own limitations. When you're over-stressed and under-rested, you aren't functioning at your best. So while you're setting up a healthy routine for the rest of your family, be sure to allow time for your own exercise, relaxation, and sleep, too.

When You Have ADHD, Too

There is about a 40% chance that at least one biological parent of a child with ADHD also has the condition. Having ADHD yourself adds another layer of complexity to your family life. The condition may affect your ability to organize your household, manage family schedules, and regulate your behavior and emotions. It may also make it more challenging to consistently apply the effective parenting strategies discussed in this book.

Many moms and dads with ADHD find that support, coaching, and therapy can help them be more effective parents. If you suspect that you might have ADHD, it's important to seek professional guidance and support for yourself, just as you would for your child.

Heather is a mom who did exactly that after her son was diagnosed with ADHD, and it dawned on her that many of his behaviors and quirks were her own. "I realized it was time to look at my own problems around this," she says. A therapist soon diagnosed Heather with ADHD, too.

Today, Heather and her son are thriving, thanks to a healthy lifestyle, therapy, and medication. But things haven't always gone so smoothly. "An ADHD household can get pretty chaotic," Heather says. "There have been times when there was a lot of stress going on in our family."

On the positive side, having ADHD herself has given Heather an insider's look at her son's world. "I believe ADHD needs to be embraced," she says. "I would encourage teens with ADHD to make peace with it, learn how they are wired, and take advantage of the creativity and uniqueness that are part of who they are."

Controlling Emotional Reactions

If you often find yourself feeling exasperated, frustrated, or angry with your teen, that's not unusual. But it's also not helpful. In fact, an angry response, such as yelling or slamming doors, tends to make teens tune out. It also models for teens ineffective ways of handling stress and conflict.

One thing that helps reduce the frustration factor is setting realistic expectations. Remember that some degree of push-back is typical for adolescents as they strive to define their identity and establish their independence. On top of that, teens with ADHD face issues with self-control, organization, and planning. So it's reasonable to expect bumps in the road.

Try not to blow things out of proportion. A failing grade on a single biology test doesn't mean that your child "will never get into college," and a lost jacket doesn't mean that your child "is so irresponsible." If these behaviors are part of a larger pattern, they may be things you need to address. But neither in itself is catastrophic, despite what your emotions might tell you.

Warning Signs to Watch For

Know how to differentiate an occasional bad day from a negative pattern that's likely to keep repeating. Some parents and teens get stuck in a destructive cycle of conflict and coercion. Typically, the chain of events goes something like this:

1. You tell your teen to do something.
2. Your teen doesn't comply.
3. You keep giving your teen the same instruction.
4. Your teen keeps ignoring you.
5. You threaten punishment.
6. Your teen responds with an angry outburst.
7. You give in, but you're not happy about it.
8. The cycle keeps repeating, but the amount of verbal aggression gradually escalates.
9. You become so emotionally overwhelmed that you pull back and stop offering feedback and supervision.

If you recognize this pattern in your relationship with your teen, it's crucial to take action to stop the downward spiral. It's especially critical to intervene if the aggression becomes physical or has the potential to do so. Expert advice from a mental health professional may be needed. With guidance and support, you can start getting your relationship back on track.

Parenting with Your Partner

The ADHD parenting journey is easier when traveled with a companion, whether that's a spouse or significant other, an ex who shares custody, another close relative, or your best friend. For the sake of brevity, we're using the term *partner* here to signify a relationship with anyone who plays a major role in helping raise your teen.

Create a culture of affirmation in your home that extends not only to your teen and any siblings but also to your partner. Just as you do with your teen, make a point of commenting on the positive, supportive things your partner does. This not only strengthens your bond with each other; it also sets an example for your teen.

All those communication skills you've been practicing with your teen come in very handy in your adult relationships as well. So put them to good use by framing concerns diplomatically, being a good listener, limiting criticism, and refraining from blame.

As far as your teen with ADHD is concerned, it's important that you and your partner be on the same page. Discuss any problems and concerns and talk over possible strategies for managing them. If your teen splits time between two homes, agree on an approach and apply it consistently. Then compare notes on how well it's working and talk about any refinements that might improve the results.

Keeping each other in the loop takes more work when you're no longer in a relationship with your teen's other parent. In some cases, you may have lingering grievances toward each other that you have to set aside for the sake your child. That's certainly not easy, but it's well worth the effort. Some issues that are particularly important to communicate with each other about include medication, behavior therapy, behavioral contracts, school, extracurricular activities, driving, dating, and curfew.

Don't just share the frustrations and worries of parenthood. Be generous about sharing the joys and successes as well. In the process, you may be surprised to realize how many things are going very well.

Key Points

- Adolescents thrive when parents are affectionate and affirming but are also willing to set and enforce rules and provide supervision.
- When choosing behaviors that you and your teen want to target for change, select ones that are positive, important, and realistic.
- By managing the consequences of your teen's actions consistently and appropriately, you can encourage a desirable behavior or discourage an undesirable one.
- Punishment is most effective when used sparingly. Aim for at least four times more positive reinforcement than punishment.

Learn More

A good place to connect with other parents is the Children and Adults with Attention-Deficit/Hyperactivity Disorder (CHADD) website (www.chadd.org/Support/attention-connection.aspx). To read about the experiences of other families living with ADHD, check out the blog section of *ADDitude* magazine's website (additudemag.com/adhdblogs).

Chapter Six

Your Teen in the Community: Fostering Friendships and Safe Choices

---

Home is still your adolescent's safe base. Yet your teen may be spending an increasing amount of time away from home, and friends may be playing a bigger role in your teen's life. That's a natural part of growing up and becoming more independent. In fact, learning how to form healthy relationships with peers is one of the core developmental tasks of adolescence.

At this age, the desire to feel like one of the gang is particularly acute. As a general rule, the bond with friends becomes closer during the adolescent years, and the identification with a particular social group or clique helps teens figure out who they are or aspire to be.

For adolescents with ADHD, however, making and keeping friends is often a challenge. Teens with ADHD tend to be less emotionally and socially mature than their peers. Plus, many have developed self-defeating behaviors, which may fall into a couple of patterns:

- The gun-shy teen. By the time they reach adolescence, many youngsters with ADHD have experienced more than their share of peer rejection or neglect. Some of these teens, especially those with the inattentive presentation of ADHD, also may be shy and anxious by nature. As a result, they may have learned to hang back in social settings. They're reluctant to initiate a conversation or invite a friend to get together outside of school.

• The pushy teen. At the other end of the spectrum, some teens with ADHD are extremely assertive, sometimes to the point of being obnoxious. They frequently initiate contact with peers, but they have trouble following through.

Even if teens with ADHD succeed in making friends, they often struggle to keep the relationship going. Trustworthiness and dependability are among the most valued traits in a friend. Although teens with ADHD may have big hearts and good intentions, many have trouble showing up reliably and doing what they say they'll do. That can be frustrating and disappointing for others, who may misread the behavior as a sign of not caring.

In addition, teens with ADHD may have difficulty taking turns, listening well, and communicating clearly. They may interrupt when other people are talking, blurt out thoughtless comments, or butt into others' activities. Those who fall short on fundamental social skills may find it hard to sustain a relationship over the long haul.

Tyler's Story

For 17-year-old Tyler, making friends in high school has proved to be difficult. "It's his biggest challenge, definitely," says his mother, Becca.

She believes that the roots of the problem reach all the way back to early childhood. "Tyler was extremely active when he was little," Becca says. "Very impulsive, very hyperactive. On a scale of 1 to 10, he was a 12." Plus, he had unusually intense fluctuations in mood, swinging from very happy to very angry to very sad.

At age five, Tyler was diagnosed with ADHD. Over the next several years, his doctor tried a variety of medication regimens, but none seemed to work for long. Over time, he got a reputation for being a troublemaker in elementary school.

Around sixth grade, however, his body's response to the medication seemed to change, leading to greater effectiveness and fewer side effects such as weight loss. On a more stable medication regimen, Tyler's behavior at school improved, but the damage to his reputation was already done. "Kids have long memories," Becca says.

Currently in 11th grade, Tyler is taking a combination of medications that is working well for him. In addition, he's seeing a therapist, and he's also working with an ADHD coach on issues such as time management. With this multifaceted approach, his ADHD and mood symptoms are under much better control than when he was younger. He's getting Bs and Cs in school, and he had a great experience with a summer job at a movie theater last year.

Yet something is still missing. "There's nobody he calls or texts with," says Becca. "I haven't let him start a Facebook page, because I'm afraid some of the other kids will be mean."

Becca knows that Tyler needs to beef up his social skills if he wants to change this situation. "He doesn't really know how to act," she says. "He'll do silly things to get attention. But put him down next to somebody and have him engage in a conversation? It doesn't happen."

The family is fortunate to live near a treatment center that offers social clubs and activities for young people with behavioral and learning differences. Tyler recently started taking part in a weekly group that plays Dungeons & Dragons. "He's having the best time," says Becca. "There are other kids like him there."

Yet she still worries about her son's ability to make and keep friends outside this structured setting. Tyler has one good friend he met at camp a while back, and Becca does what she can to nurture the relationship. Because the friend lives 45 minutes away and Tyler doesn't drive yet, that includes providing transportation. "I make the drive at least once a month," says Becca. "It's a long way to go, but I think it means a lot to Tyler."

Peer Neglect, Rejection, and Bullying

Social interactions are a two-way street. A teen with ADHD may behave in ways that make it harder to forge lasting friendships. In response, the teen's peers may act in ways that only exacerbate the problem. Possible responses may include neglect, rejection, and bullying.

Peer Neglect

In some cases, peers ignore the teen with ADHD. They leave the teen out of conversations, and they don't think to save the teen a seat or invite him or her to parties. This can lead to feelings of isolation and loneliness.

Typically, teens with ADHD who are neglected by their peers are inattentive, quiet, and anxious. They have a tendency to fade into the background, making them easy to ignore. Not all neglected teens fit this profile, however. Those who are overly pushy or whose behavior is annoying may also end up being excluded.

Peer Rejection

At times, peers actively rebuff the social overtures of the teen with ADHD. They may make rude or insensitive comments. Repeated rejection can be demoralizing and may lead to low self-esteem. In some cases, it could contribute to depression.

Teens with ADHD who are rejected by their peers are often hyperactive, overly talkative, and impulsive. Their behavior may be considered obnoxious. But that's not always the case. Quieter teens who are perceived as being different or not fitting in may be rejected, too.

Standing Up to Stigma

There is no reason for your child to ever feel like a "bad kid" for having ADHD. And there's no reason for you to ever feel like a "poor parent" because your child has a brain-based condition. Yet, fair or not, false but hurtful stereotypes about ADHD still exist.

Talk with your teen about when and with whom to disclose a diagnosis of ADHD. There are varying degrees of transparency. Some teens place a premium on privacy and prefer to talk about ADHD only with family members, teachers, doctors, and their closest friends. Others highly value openness and are comfortable discussing ADHD with a wide range of friends and acquaintances. There is no single right or wrong approach to this issue.

If your teen prefers to be more private than public, honor that wish. Just be clear that it's not a matter of hiding something embarrassing or shameful. Rather, it's a matter of respecting your teen's personal preference.

Realize that most people who say hurtful things are acting out of ignorance rather than malice. When you do talk about ADHD, use it as an opportunity to educate others. Teach your teen to treat everyone with the same empathy and acceptance that he or she would like to receive in return. Your child will grow up kinder and wiser for the experience.

Bullying by Peers

In some cases, peers cross the line into bully territory. Bullying occurs when another person or group repeatedly acts aggressively toward someone seen as being weaker. Teens with ADHD may be the target of various forms of bullying:

- Verbal bullying. This involves saying or writing mean-spirited things. It may take the form of teasing, name-calling, taunting, unwanted sexual comments, or verbal threats.
- Social bullying. This involves damaging the teen's reputation or relationships. It may take the form of spreading nasty rumors, embarrassing the teen in public, or telling other people not to be friends with the teen.
- Physical bullying. This includes both inflicting bodily harm and damaging the teen's possessions. It may take the form of shoving, tripping, hitting, kicking, or pinching. Or it may involve taking away or intentionally breaking something that belongs to the teen.
- Cyberbullying. This refers to bullying via electronic technology. It often takes the form of mean-spirited comments, hurtful rumors, or embarrassing photos or videos, which may be texted, emailed, or posted on social media sites. Another form of cyberbullying involves creating a fake online profile for the teen, which is intended to hurt the teen's reputation or elicit unwelcome responses.

Factors that heighten the risk of being bullied include being perceived as different, having low self-esteem, being depressed or anxious, having few friends, and being seen as annoying or provoking. These are all common traits in teens with ADHD, so it's no surprise that such teens have an increased chance of being targeted by bullies.

Of course, not all kids with ADHD are picked on or pushed around. But just in case, be alert for possible warning signs. Some teens will ask for help directly. Others, however, may be reluctant to talk about what's going on. They may feel helpless and humiliated, or they may fear further rejection and retaliation if they tell anyone.

Unexplained injuries are an obvious red flag. Often, however, the warning signs are subtler. Teens who previously liked school or an after-school activity may suddenly not want to go. They may experience a loss of friends or plummet in grades. Or they may come home with their clothing, books, or electronics damaged and not be able to clearly explain to you what happened.

Some teens who are being bullied develop new problems with insomnia or changes in appetite. They may have headaches or stomach aches for which the doctor can't find a medical reason. At times, they may begin behaving in self-destructive ways—for example, by running away, harming themselves, or talking about suicide.

Such changes in behavior don't always mean that your teen is being bullied, but they do signal distress. Don't ignore the warning signs. Reach out for help to your child's doctor, therapist, teacher, or school counselor right away. To learn more about preventing, recognizing, and responding to bullying, visit stopbullying.gov.

When Your Teen Is the Aggressor

It's also possible for teens with ADHD to go the opposite direction and become the aggressor. The aggressive behavior may follow a couple of different patterns:

- Reactive aggression. Some teens with ADHD, especially those with the impulsive form, have trouble controlling their emotional reactions. When they feel frustrated or things don't go their way, they may react by losing their temper. They might yell, curse, slam doors, throw things, or strike out physically. Let your teen's treatment providers know if you're seeing this type of aggressive behavior. It needs to be addressed as part of the overall treatment plan for managing ADHD.

- Being a bully. Other teens engage in aggressive behavior that is more calculated and aimed at taking advantage of someone perceived as weaker. In other words, they become bullies. This goes beyond ADHD itself. It's an additional problem, particularly common in teens with ADHD who also have conduct disorder. Both ADHD and the bullying behavior need to be addressed by treatment providers.

Keep in mind that bullies aren't always physically bigger and stronger than their targets. They may see themselves as more powerful than their targets, based on other characteristics, such as popularity, intelligence, toughness, or parental wealth.

Bullying hurts those on both the giving and the receiving end. Research shows that kids who bully others are more likely than non-bullies to

- Abuse alcohol and drugs
- Get into fights
- Vandalize property
- Drop out of school
- Be sexually active at a young age

If bullying isn't dealt with now, the problems can persist into adulthood. Bullies have an increased risk of growing into adults who are abusive toward their romantic partners or children. They're also more likely to be convicted of crimes as adults. So it's crucial to seek help if you believe your teen is being a bully. Talk with your teen's doctor or a mental health professional.

Supporting Healthy Peer Relationships

It's important to be aware of the social hurdles that your teen with ADHD might face. But it's equally important to remember that young people with ADHD have the potential to establish friendships and form healthy relationships. These things may take extra effort, especially for some teens with ADHD, but the effort is likely to be well rewarded.

Research has shown that the ability to make and maintain close friendships is a protective factor in adolescence. It helps teens thrive in their lives today, and it encourages them to grow into caring, responsible adults in the future. In contrast, children and teens who lack strong friendships are more likely to develop low self-esteem, have poor grades, drop out of school, and run afoul of the law.

You can help your teen develop the skills needed for forming friendships. By practicing good listening and clear communication at home and by setting a respectful tone within your family, you're teaching your teen how to build a healthy relationship. Your teen can then apply what has been learned to all types of relationships, including friendships. Beyond that, these are some other things you can do to nurture your teen's social skills:

- Welcome your teen's friends into your home. Encourage your teen to invite friends over and provide a safe, comfortable space for the kids to hang out.

- Offer some subtle social coaching. Be available to suggest possible activities or gently nudge the friendship along, especially in the early stages.
- Get acquainted with your teen's friends. Strike up a conversation as you're driving the school carpool or having your teen's friends over for dinner.
- Include friends in outings. If you plan to take your teen to the mall, to a ballgame, or out for pizza night, suggest inviting a friend to come along.
- Get to know the friend's family. Consider planning a backyard cookout or bowling night where both families, including the teens, can get together.

How Involved Should You Be?

When your child was younger, you may have found it relatively easy to pick up the phone, call another parent, and set up a play date. Now that your child is an adolescent, however, facilitating your child's friendships is a more complicated matter. While it's still critical to stay involved in your child's life, it's also important to respect your teen's growing need for privacy and independence. Balancing these two competing objectives is tricky, but it can be done.

Be prepared for a few challenging moments. Parental involvement in a teen's social life can be complicated and uncomfortable at times. Consequently, many parents have a tendency to back away and not get involved. But this can be a mistake, because adolescents, especially those with ADHD, need the support and guidance of their parents to deal with peer relationships.

Rather than backing away, approach this situation from the standpoint of an authoritative parent (described in Chapter Five). Be encouraging and available, but not smothering.

Understand that it's normal for your teen not to want you hovering all the time, especially when friends are around. If you're being too intrusive, your teen may ask you to butt out. Try not to take it personally and give your teen some breathing room.

On the other hand, you still need to monitor what's going on. You should always have a good idea of who your teen is hanging out with, where they are, and what they're doing. When the kids are at your place, check in on them now and then. Be aware of what's happening under your own roof, and don't be afraid to set and enforce house rules for acceptable behavior.

Teen Dating and ADHD

For parents, it may be hard to imagine their children having romantic or sexual feelings. For teens themselves, however, it's sometimes difficult to think about anything else! Whether you're ready for it or not, dating is likely to be on your adolescent's mind. It's better to accept this reality than to pretend it doesn't exist.

When an adolescent has ADHD, those first dating relationships are often fraught with extra challenges. An inattentive teen who is a poor listener may come off as uninterested. An impulsive teen may blurt out tactless comments. And a disorganized teen who doesn't show up on time may not get a second chance.

The help you give your teen with managing ADHD, improving listening, practicing communication, and developing social skills will carry over to this area of life. In addition, here are some specific ways you can help:

- Facilitate group activities that give teens a chance to mingle. That might mean volunteering to help out with a school dance, church social, or neighborhood 5K run. Or it might simply mean getting together with a few other parents to organize pizza and a movie for a group of friends.

- Coordinate transportation to and from activities with other parents. This helps ensure that everyone gets picked up on time and dropped off where they're supposed to be. When it's time for the return trip, having a parent provide transportation helps ensure that everyone is back home by curfew time.

- Have "the talk"—not only about sexual mechanics, but also about your family's values. Talk about the sexual choices and pressures that teens may face and discuss ways to handle them effectively. Don't make it just a one-time conversation, either. Instead, think of it as an ongoing dialogue. Let your teen know that you're always available to discuss things, openly and honestly. If you've already established the habit of communication with your teen, it's much easier to have ongoing conversations about dating relationships.

Promoting Smart Choices, Preventing Health Risks

Sexual activity is just one of several issues about which adolescents are called upon to make serious, sometimes life-changing, decisions. Adolescents are also likely to confront choices about alcohol, drugs, and smoking.

This is treacherous territory for any teen to navigate. But for teens with ADHD, the risks are magnified. Those whose ADHD is characterized by impulsivity are prone to spur-of-the-moment decisions, which they may later come to regret. Those who have conduct disorder along with ADHD are especially likely to flout rules, break laws, and engage in destructive behavior.

Yet having ADHD doesn't mean your adolescent is destined for trouble. There's a lot you can do to help guide your teen safely through the minefield of growing up.

The Influence of Peers

When you hear the phrase "peer pressure," you probably think of it as a negative force. But peers can also be a positive influence. It all depends on the company your adolescent keeps.

Studies by psychologists such as Thomas Berndt have confirmed what generations of parents have observed: Friends exert a significant influence on the attitudes and behavior of young people. Over time, adolescents and their friends tend to become increasingly similar in how they think and behave.

That can be either a good thing or a bad thing. Yes, your child probably knows some young people whose behavior is troubled. But chances are, your child also knows teens who are making good grades, working hard at sports practice, volunteering for community projects, and doing chores for aging relatives.

Talk with your teen about the importance of choosing one's friends wisely. Encourage picking friends who generally make good choices and have like-minded values. But be realistic: You can't keep your teen in a cocoon. So make sure to also have periodic conversations about how to handle situations in which friends are disregarding rules or doing things that go against your teen's personal values. One rule of thumb you might want to pass along: "If something feels wrong for you, it probably is."

Discuss the societal pressures that teens often face, and talk about ways to handle them. For example, let's say the two of you are discussing what to do if your teen is at a party where underage drinking is going on. You could rehearse saying "no," simply and decisively, without having to justify that position. If your teen chooses to explain to close friends, you could practice short, to-the-point explanations that don't invite argument (for example, "I'm in training for [a sport]"). And you could agree on a code phrase that your teen can use to call you for a ride home without losing face.

Present the facts about the risks of alcohol, drugs, smoking, and unprotected sex. Make your expectations clear. Listen to your teen's concerns as well, and let your teen know that you're always available to answer questions or discuss dilemmas as they arise.

Schools, family support groups, and community organizations sometimes offer talks for parents on promoting healthy choices by adolescents. Sign up, if an opportunity comes along. You might also want to share these online resources with your teen and use them as a springboard for conversation:

- Drug abuse prevention: teens.drugabuse.gov (National Institute on Drug Abuse)
- Smoking prevention: teen.smokefree.gov (National Cancer Institute)
- Teen pregnancy prevention: stayteen.org (National Campaign to Prevent Teen and Unplanned Pregnancy)
- Underage drinking prevention: thecoolspot.gov (National Institute on Alcohol Abuse and Alcoholism); toosmart-tostart.samhsa.gov (Substance Abuse and Mental Health Services Administration)

Talking About Alcohol and Drugs

Underage drinking and experimentation with drugs are very common among adolescents, and the pressure to partake can be intense. It's a mistake to ignore that reality. The key to helping your teen make smart choices is staying involved while respecting your teen's autonomy.

Help your teen navigate this tricky terrain by inviting frank discussion. It's important for your teen to understand the legal, health, and psychological risks associated with alcohol and drug use, as well as your family's values around these issues.

At the same time, it's critical for parents to communicate an understanding of the challenges teens face in this arena. If your teen responds by sharing something personal, listen in an empathic and nonjudgmental manner. Alcohol and drug use can be difficult issues to discuss, but don't shy away from talking about them. Instead, address the subject in the context of ongoing communication and problem-solving with your teen.

Your Influence Matters, Too

It all comes back to a strong relationship with you. That's the bedrock on which the rest of your teen's relationships are built. When you get into the habit of having frequent, brief conversations with your teen, you'll find that more opportunities arise to reinforce positive messages.

While you're discussing house rules, the conversation may segue into the health risks of substance abuse. While you're chatting about getting together with friends, the conversation may turn toward choosing supportive friends and dealing with negative peer pressure. Take advantage of these natural conversational openings to revisit important subjects. Focus on being a good listener, and work hard to understand the intentions and feelings behind the words your teen is using.

Don't feel as if you have to discuss everything in a single conversation. Aim to end your chats before your teen starts tuning you out. You can always continue the discussion at later time.

Helping Your Teen Find Success in Sports and Clubs

For many young people, being part of a sports team, drama club, school band, church youth group, or other after-school organization turns out to be one of the highlights of their teen years. Such groups offer adolescents a chance to have fun with peers in an adult-supervised environment. These are some of the benefits of extracurricular group activities:

- Sense of achievement. Teens with ADHD who struggle in school can often find an after-school activity in which they're able to shine. This opportunity to experience success is a boost to their self-esteem.
- Growth in self-discipline. Some teens with ADHD thrive in structured physical activities that place a premium on hard work and self-discipline, such as team sports, martial arts, or ballet. These activities give them a chance to practice self-control while having the freedom to move their bodies.
- Peer interactions. Through sports, clubs, and youth groups, teens with ADHD are able to engage with peers in meaningful ways. They get to practice their social skills and bond with peers over a mutual interest. Plus, they have opportunities to form friendships that may be critical for them across many areas of their lives.
- Mentor relationships. Extracurricular activities also bring teens into contact with adult coaches and group leaders, who may serve as mentors and role models. Research shows that having supportive relationships with adults outside the family helps promote healthy development in adolescence.

Finding the Right Activity

Help your teen find an extracurricular activity that's a good match for his or her interests and talents. That might be soccer, basketball, or cheerleading, or it might be choir, chess club, or the school newspaper. In addition to the activity itself, consider the participants. Look for a peer group with whom your teen feels comfortable.

Advise your teen not to overschedule with too many commitments and competing priorities. For a teen with ADHD who has difficulty managing time and organizing activities, an overstuffed schedule can be quite stressful. And for a teen who already has trouble getting homework and studying done, having too many non-school activities pulling attention in other directions may just make the problem worse.

On the other hand, under-scheduling can be a problem, too. Teens who don't have any extracurricular activities at all are missing out on valuable benefits. Unfortunately, teens with ADHD—especially those who've had discouraging experiences in the past—sometimes have learned to shy away from getting involved in such activities.

This is another way in which you can help. Let your teen know you understand how he or she feels. But make it clear that doing nothing but sitting at home and playing electronic games isn't an option. Offer to help identify a few possible activities. They should be meaningful and of high interest for your teen, as well as affordable and accessible for your family. Then give your teen the final word on which extracurricular activity to sign up for.

Keep an open mind about the possibilities. For example, some teens with ADHD struggle with team sports that require sustained attention to what several players are doing at once, such as soccer, softball, and basketball. However, the same teens sometimes do well in team sports based on individual events, such as swimming, track, and gymnastics. The "best" activity is the one at which your teen has fun and feels successful.

Benefits of Physical Exercise

Kids ages 6 through 17 should aim for at least an hour of physical activity every day, according to the Centers for Disease Control and Prevention. That includes not only organized sports and exercise programs, but also physical activities such as walking to school, riding a bike, or mowing the lawn. Fewer than 30% of high school students meet this goal.

One way for your teen to get more physical activity is by signing up for a sports team or exercise class. Staying active is terrific for your teen's overall health. It helps boost cardiovascular fitness, control weight, increase endurance, and build strong muscles and bones. Plus, regular physical activity has psychological benefits that may be particularly valuable for teens with ADHD, including enhanced self-esteem and reduced anxiety and stress.

Does exercise also have a direct impact on ADHD itself? There's mounting evidence to support this idea. In animals, research shows that exercise can enhance the development and function of areas in the brain that are believed to be affected by ADHD. In children and teens with ADHD, studies suggest that aerobic exercise (such as brisk walking, running, and swimming laps) may improve planning, attention, and impulse control. Although the effects of aerobic activity have generally been shown to be modest, when used in combination with behavioral strategies and, if needed, medication, physical activity can be part of a comprehensive intervention plan.

Teaming Up with Coaches and Group Leaders

In adolescence, it's normal for your teen's social circle to expand further beyond the family. You (and your partner, if any) are still by far the biggest adult influence on your teen's life. But a sports coach, youth group leader, music teacher, or other adult mentor may serve as an additional source of adult guidance and support.

Adolescents typically don't want their parents to be at the center of every extracurricular activity, and that's normal, too. You can respect this wish and still keep tabs on what your teen is doing. Get to know the coach or group leader in a natural, unobtrusive way. Reassure yourself that this is someone who is competent and trustworthy. Then sit back and let the coach do the coaching or the group leader do the leading.

You have your own role to fill as your teen's number one fan. Whenever possible, show up for games, recitals, plays, and other events. Teens notice and appreciate their parents' presence, whether or not they let on that they do. By being there, you also have a chance to observe how your teen interacts with the grown-ups in charge.

Many teams and youth groups rely on parent volunteers for a variety of jobs, from organizing fundraisers to collecting tickets. Volunteer when your schedule allows. This shows your support, and it's often a good way to get better acquainted with the coach or group leader. Plus, it gives you a chance to meet some of the other parents, and that may lead to social opportunities for your teen down the road.

When ADHD Causes Problems

At times, you may believe that ADHD is affecting your teen's behavior or performance in an extracurricular activity. In most cases, it's best to talk things over with your teen. If you go straight to the coach or group leader with your concern, your teen may feel as if you've betrayed a confidence. That's likely to lead to anger and resentment rather than constructive change.

Plus, if your teen feels that the coach or group leader is in cahoots with you, that could damage your child's relationship with this individual.

Instead, talk with your teen about the problem you've noticed and possible ways of managing it. In some cases, your teen may be able to identify and make behavioral changes that resolve the issue without needing to involve anyone else. In other cases, however, you may think it beneficial for the coach or group leader to be brought into the loop. To broach the subject with your teen, you might say something like: "I wonder if it would be helpful for the coach to know that you have ADHD and it can be difficult for you to [do something specific]."

If your teen demurs, respect that. You can bring up the suggestion again at a later time. If your teen agrees to a conversation with the coach or group leader, be sensitive to your teen's privacy. Take the coach or group leader aside where there are no other kids or parents around or set up a private conference time. Ideally, your teen should be there, too. Encourage your teen to play an active role in the discussion.

Driving with ADHD: A Unique Challenge

Nothing symbolizes the newfound freedom and responsibility of late adolescence more than a driver's license. For any teen, being handed the car keys for the first time is a heady experience. But for your teen with ADHD, the excitement is tempered by some sobering realities.

Among drivers in general, the rate of traffic accidents is higher in 16- to 19-year-olds than in older age groups. In fact, per mile driven, teen drivers are nearly three times as likely as drivers ages 20 and up to be in a fatal crash.

Having ADHD in addition to being a young, inexperienced driver only compounds the risk. Compared to peers without the condition, teen drivers with ADHD are especially at risk for the following:

- Citations for traffic violations or reckless driving
- Suspended or revoked driver's license
- Motor vehicle accidents in general
- Traffic accidents resulting in injury or death
- Hit-and-run traffic accidents

The risks shouldn't be taken lightly. Yet it's worth remembering that there are also many young drivers with ADHD who have clean driving records and don't get into accidents. The key is to set conditions for getting a license. Then, when your teen is ready, use proven strategies to teach safe driving practices.

How ADHD Affects Driving

The first step is understanding how ADHD may influence your teen's driving behavior. Several factors may come into play:

- Distractibility. Among drivers involved in fatal crashes, teens are more likely than older drivers to be distracted at the time of the accident. Teens with ADHD are at especially high risk, because they often have more trouble resisting distractions than peers without ADHD. Distractions can take numerous forms, including texting, using a phone, operating a navigation system, adjusting a radio or MP3 player, talking to passengers, and eating behind the wheel.

- Impulsivity. Teens whose ADHD is characterized by impulsivity may be more willing to take risks while driving, increasing the chance of driver error.
- Difficulty anticipating hazards. Some teens with ADHD are poor at planning, so they may have difficulty thinking ahead about potential hazards on the road.
- Unrealistic self-assessment. Teens with ADHD often have an unrealistic view of their own abilities, which could lead to not being cautious enough.
- Substance abuse. Driving under the influence of alcohol or drugs greatly increases the risk of getting into an accident. Teens with ADHD generally are more likely than their peers without the condition to abuse alcohol or drugs, and teens with disruptive behavior problems in combination with ADHD are especially prone to substance abuse. When teens with ADHD drink and drive, their driving may be even more severely impaired than that of peers who don't have ADHD.

Talk with your teen about the challenges of driving with ADHD. Rather than lecturing, engage your teen in a dialogue. Be realistically encouraging. Express hope that your teen can learn to be a safe driver through self-awareness, hard work, and help from others.

Keeping Your Teen Driver Safe on the Road

Graduated driver licensing is a system by which young drivers gain experience behind the wheel in a gradual way designed to reduce risk. All 50 states and the District of Columbia have some form of graduated licensing system. Although specifics vary, this type of system has three stages:

1. A supervised learning stage
2. A restricted license, granted after passing a road test, which requires supervision to drive in certain situations (for example, with teen passengers or at night)
3. An unrestricted license

Conditions for Learning to Drive

When your teen is old enough and wants to start supervised learning, sit down together and create a behavioral contract. At the Center for Management of ADHD at The Children's Hospital of Philadelphia, Dr. Power recommends that parents and teens outline the conditions that must be met before teens begin the process. Here are some conditions you may want to include:

- No evidence of alcohol or drug use. You may also want to add no tobacco use, because this, too, is a sign of being a responsible person with regard to making healthy choices.
- Acceptable grades in school. Some teens with ADHD have learning challenges and may need special supports in school. Taking these challenges and supports into account, set some reasonable academic expectations for your teen.
- Pattern of meeting curfew. Getting home on time is another sign of being a responsible person. It's further evidence that your teen is ready to handle the freedom of driving.
- Willingness to consider medication. Your teen should be willing to discuss treatment options with the doctor and weigh the pros and cons of medication with an open mind. If your teen agrees to use medication, then he or she should consistently take it as prescribed. If your teen decides not to take medication, then he or she needs to agree to additional behavioral strategies.

- Cooperation with behavioral contract discussions. Your teen should be willing to negotiate behavioral contracts with you. Plus, your teen should have a good track record for fulfilling the contracts.

Conditions for Getting a License

When your teen wants to get a restricted license, it's time for added responsibilities. Along with continuing to meet the previous conditions, your teen should meet criteria such as these:

- Understanding of state traffic laws
- Extended training on the road
- Agreement to not use a cell phone while driving

The last point is crucial, because cell phone use is a major cause of distracted driving. In addition, there are legal ramifications. As of mid-2016, texting while driving had been banned for young drivers in 48 states and the District of Columbia. Any other use of cell phones was also restricted for novice drivers in three-fourths of states and D.C.

To monitor compliance, some parents and teens agree to use cell phone blocking technology. This involves installing an app on the teen's phone that disables specific features, such as texting, while the vehicle is moving. If you decide to use this type of technology, choose an app that activates automatically when your teen is driving. Some apps can be configured to send you an alert if your teen turns the app off.

Conditions for Earning Driving Privileges

Once your adolescent is ready to move on to an unrestricted driver's license, it's time to revisit what the privilege of driving entails. Review the contract that the two of you created earlier, and stress that the same conditions still apply.

Set up a menu of rewards for following the contract. For example, the contract might stipulate that, if all criteria are met for a specified time period, your teen can earn more driving time or an allowance for gas money.

As a rule, Dr. Power does not recommend buying a car for a teen who is a novice driver, even if you can afford it. For a 16- or 17-year-old, few things are more reinforcing than the privilege to drive. Having your child work to gain access to the family car underscores that it's a privilege to be earned through responsible behavior. In contrast, when your child has unlimited access to a car of his or her own, that doesn't send the same strong message.

Setting a Good Example

Finally, one of the best ways to help your teen become a safe driver is by being a good role model. So put down your phone, buckle up your seat belt, stay within the speed limit, use your turn signals, and drive defensively. In short, drive exactly the way you would like your teen to drive when you aren't around.

You can make some of this modeling more explicit by thinking out loud. Now and then, when you're behind the wheel and your teen is a passenger, talk to yourself about what you're doing and why; for example, "I'm not sure that car is going to stop, so I'm going to be careful here." At first, it might feel a bit odd to provide play-by-play commentary for your own driving, but doing so may help your teen pick up the safe driving maneuver that you're demonstrating.

With time and effort, many teens with ADHD go on to become excellent drivers. Eighteen-year-old Hannah, first diagnosed with ADHD in fourth grade, is a case in point. Over the years, Hannah has sometimes struggled with issues such as turning in schoolwork on time and acting rebellious at home. "But she loves her freedom, so she has worked very hard at driving," says her mother. "She has never had an accident, and she's actually a better driver than her older sister [who doesn't have ADHD]. Driving has become an area of strength for her."

Key Points

- Adolescents with ADHD have an increased risk of being ignored, rejected, or bullied by their peers.
- Participation in extracurricular group activities often leads to positive peer interactions and mentorship relationships. Such activities may also boost self-esteem and self-discipline.
- Teen drivers with ADHD are at particularly high risk for traffic citations and motor vehicle accidents.
- By establishing sensible ground rules for learning to drive, getting a license, and earning driving privileges, you can reduce the risks.

Learn More

Read more about the types of experiences, relationships, and behaviors that help adolescents thrive on the Search Institute website (search-institute.org).

Chapter Seven

Your Teen at School: Promoting Smart Learning and Study Strategies

By middle school and high school, most students with ADHD are able to sit in a desk without running and jumping around the classroom. They are able to raise a hand before speaking up in class (or all too often, they have learned not to speak at all). But that doesn't necessarily mean that having ADHD is less of a challenge.

In fact, the further along students are in their education, the more organized and self-directed they are expected to be. It's assumed that middle-schoolers and high-schoolers can keep track of their assignments, manage their study time, and plan ahead for the completion of big projects. Living up to these high expectations can be difficult for any student, but it can be particularly challenging for a teen with ADHD.

Compounding the difficulty, students this age generally have multiple teachers, rather than just one or two as they did in early elementary school. That means adapting to multiple teaching styles and differing class requirements. Adults who work with multiple clients, each with different demands and deadlines, often find this arrangement quite challenging and stressful. So it's no surprise that some teens—particularly those who have specific difficulties with attention and organization—would find it overwhelming.

With a typical class period lasting less than an hour per day, there are also fewer opportunities for teachers and students to get to know one another well. Yet a strong student–teacher relationship is a powerful protective factor. Vulnerable students, including those with ADHD, may have the most to lose if they are unable to form a strong, positive relationship with at least one of their teachers.

At the same time, the teachers often are dealing with their own set of demands. Under pressure to focus on specific learning objectives, some occasionally lose sight of the whole student. This, too, can work to the detriment of students with ADHD.

Yet, despite these potential pitfalls, there is much to be optimistic about. The majority of teachers have a deep commitment to helping students reach their potential. Today, a growing number of teachers combine that dedication with a solid grounding in knowledge about ADHD. Many derive great satisfaction from finding ways to connect with a previously tuned-out student and helping that student succeed.

Often, students with ADHD benefit from small changes in classroom techniques or materials that help them work around their challenges. Some qualify for more extensive or intensive special education services. In this chapter, we'll discuss classroom accommodations and educational planning for middle school and high school students. (The needs of college students with ADHD are addressed in the next chapter.)

Realistically, however, when your teen has six or seven different teachers, there are limits to what any single teacher can do. So there's also a need for interventions that go beyond the individual classroom. We'll look at some successful interventions that use school-based mentors to help students stay on top of all their schoolwork.

Finally, *you* play an important role in your teen's success at school, just as you do in other facets of your child's life. From encouraging good homework habits at home to advocating for your child at meetings with school staff, there's a lot you can do to help your teen have a better school experience. We'll offer tips on that here as well.

Abbie's Story

Bob is a great example of the supportive role that an empathetic parent can play. He's not only the father of two young adult children with ADHD. In his forties, he was also diagnosed with ADHD himself, so he has a window into his children's world.

His daughter Abbie, now 20, has both ADHD and dyslexia, a learning disorder that impairs the ability to read and spell. As a teen, she would often talk with her dad about the frustration she felt at school. Bob recalls those conversations going something like this:

> ABBIE: How come I work harder than anybody in class, and kids who don't even care always do better than I do?
> BOB: Well, that's not really true. There are things you excel at. But you'll always have to work harder at some things.
> ABBIE: But it gets better, right?
> BOB: You get more used to it, and you get more used to the amount of effort you have to put in. And you learn to appreciate the other gifts you have.

According to Bob, one of Abbie's gifts is a highly developed sense of intuition, which feeds her creativity. Today, Abbie is an art major on the verge of completing an associate's degree.

After that, she plans to transfer to another college, where she hopes to pursue a Master of Fine Arts degree. From a girl who once doubted her own ability to measure up in school, she has blossomed into a self-assured young woman.

"Now she's very education focused, and she's self-aware about ADHD," says Bob. "She has learned what she needs to do to stay on track. If there's something she wants bad enough, she's willing to work hard to get it."

Teacher Strategies that Promote Academic Success

Even for dedicated, experienced educators, teaching a student with ADHD can be a challenge at times. However, research has shown that certain teaching strategies increase the odds of success. The strategies listed here are fundamental to good teaching in any situation, but they're especially beneficial when a student has ADHD:

- Building on what's already known. Imagine yourself in a graduate-level class on a subject you know nothing about, be it particle physics or Elizabethan literature. How long do you think you could stay focused on the lecture before your mind began to wander? If you're like most people, the answer is "not very long." Students may feel overwhelmed and tune out if they're hit with too much new information at once. As a rule of thumb, about 80% of instructional material should already be familiar, so that only about 20% of what's being presented is new. Teachers need to make sure students have enough background information before introducing new lessons.

- Highlighting the key points. The best teachers talk almost in outlines. They make sure that the main points stand out, much like an outline's top-level headings. To draw attention to a main idea, the teacher might restate it several times using slightly different words, write it on the board, act it out, or use it as the caption for a cartoon. Each main point has a few secondary points that get a little less emphasis, much like the subheadings on an outline's second level. Supporting details get even less emphasis, similar to the items on an outline's third level.

- Getting students actively involved. Good teachers don't just stand in front of the class and talk nonstop for 45 minutes. Instead, they engage every student in conversation through strategic, open-ended questions. They also encourage students to engage with each other in partner or small-group activities.

- Giving students a choice. A teacher might let students choose a class project or activity from a few different options. Students are more engaged and their behavior improves when they have some control over what they do.

- Setting behavioral expectations. The classroom should have a few key rules, and they should be stated clearly. Some teachers post them so there's no ambiguity about which behaviors are acceptable and which are not.

- Providing positive feedback. The most effective teachers don't emphasize wrong answers or unacceptable conduct. Instead, they go out of their way to identify and provide positive reinforcement for accurate answers and responsible behavior, and they provide specific, constructive recommendations.

Planning Next Year's Schedule

Unless you work in your child's school district, you likely will have limited opportunities to observe the teachers in your child's school. But you can learn a lot by conferring with friends who work in the district or who have had children with ADHD attend the school.

Talk with your teen as well as other parents and students to gain insight into the instructional strategies used by different teachers. If there is an ADHD family support group in your area, that may be a good place to get the inside scoop from parents whose children have needs similar to your teen's. Then keep this information in mind when it's time to sit down with your teen and select next year's courses.

If you've noticed that certain teaching strategies are especially helpful for your teen, you may want to mention this to your teen's academic advisor. You might get a better response if you frame a request in terms of asking for the specific teaching approaches your teen needs, rather than asking for a particular teacher by name. It's usually best to make this type of request in late spring when schools are doing their schedule planning.

The Power of a Good Student–Teacher Relationship

Research has shown that students are more motivated to learn and more engaged in the process when they have a good relationship with the teacher. They also tend to perform better academically and relate more effectively to peers.

So what does a strong student–teacher relationship look like? Let's say a student has just earned a black belt in martial arts, had a painting picked for a community art show, or landed a coveted summer job. If the student is eager to tell the teacher, that's a sign that he or she knows the teacher is genuinely interested and will share the student's excitement about this success.

Or take a situation when things aren't going so well. Let's say a student is being bullied and teased by kids outside of class. If the student is willing to seek advice from the teacher, that's a sign that he or she trusts the teacher to listen and offer help rather than brushing off the concerns or making the student feel belittled.

Some teachers are especially skilled at connecting with their students, including those kids who may take some extra effort to get to know. Common characteristics of teachers who are skillful relationship builders include the following:

- Calling students by their names
- Spending some class time getting to know each student individually
- Expressing interest in students' outside interests and after-school activities
- Showing warmth and respect to each student in class
- Creating a positive, encouraging, inclusive atmosphere in the classroom
- Avoiding showing anger, frustration, or irritation
- Avoiding using sarcasm or making snide remarks

Teachers who are good relationship builders can have a profound impact on the lives of their students. This is especially true for students with ADHD, some of whom unfortunately arrive at middle school and high school with a string of negative school experiences behind them. So be supportive of any positive relationships that your teen forms with teachers, and let these caring teachers know how much you appreciate them.

Understanding Accommodations, 504 Plans, and IEPs

Many students with ADHD benefit from changes in the classroom that help them work around their learning and behavioral issues. When discussing these kinds of changes with school personnel, you may hear the term *accommodations*. This term refers to changes in classroom techniques or materials that are designed to level the playing field for a student with ADHD, much the way eyeglasses do for a student with poor vision.

A student who receives accommodations generally is required to learn the same content and meet the same expectations as classmates, but adjustments are made to compensate for the impact of the disability on school performance. For example, a student with ADHD might be seated near the front of the class, given a quiet space for taking tests, and provided with an extra set of textbooks to keep at home.

In contrast, *modifications* are adjustments to what is learned. The amount of content may be reduced or expectations may be different than for other students. For example, a student with dyslexia as well as ADHD might take an alternative English class in which readings and tests are written three grade levels below the student's actual grade.

Another term you might hear is *interventions*, which refers to a set of strategies designed through a systematic process to improve student skills, performance, or behavior. One example might be a behavioral contract negotiated by the student, teacher, and parent. Another might be working with a reading tutor to supplement the reading curriculum.

In many cases, accommodations, modifications, or well-planned, targeted interventions are beneficial. As a general rule, it is advisable to hold students to similar expectations as their peers and to emphasize skill development to meet these expectations, as opposed to lowering standards to make it easier for students to succeed. These strategies may be formalized in a written educational plan, which can take one of two forms: a 504 plan or an Individualized Education Program (IEP).

504 Plan

A 504 plan is commonly used to ensure that essential accommodations and services are implemented for students with disabilities, including those with ADHD. This type of plan is based on Section 504 of the Rehabilitation Act of 1973, a federal civil rights law that prohibits discrimination on the basis of disability. To qualify for a 504 plan, your child must have a disability that substantially limits the ability to learn and participate in the classroom.

A 504 evaluation may be initiated either by you or by the school. If it's determined that your child is eligible, a 504 plan is created by a group of people who are familiar with your child's needs and educational options. The makeup of this group, known as a 504 committee, can vary. Typically, however, your teen's 504 committee might include general and special education teachers, other school personnel, you, and possibly your child. Just keep in mind: The law doesn't mandate that parents have a seat at the table for 504 meetings, so you may sometimes need to be assertive about requesting to be included.

The law also doesn't specify exactly what a 504 plan must contain. At a minimum, it should state which accommodations or services will be provided to your child and by whom. It should also name the person responsible for making sure the plan is followed.

Be aware that the way in which 504 plans are implemented can vary widely from state to state, and even from school district to school district within the same state. Get to know how things work in your state and school district. In addition to talking with school personnel, ask around among other parents at the school who know the ropes. Your local Parent Training and Information Center may be a good source of information (see the box Educate Yourself on Navigating the System). Other helpful resources include Education Law Centers, which are found in some states, such as New Jersey (edlawcenter.org) and Pennsylvania (elc-pa.org).

If you disagree with your child's 504 plan or the way it's being implemented, ask for a meeting with the school to voice your concerns. It's always best when you can hash out an agreement through discussion and negotiation. But if that doesn't work, you may seek mediation or an impartial hearing. If you believe that the school has repeatedly failed to comply with anti-discrimination law, you may want to look into filing a discrimination complaint with the Office for Civil Rights (OCR) for the U.S. Department of Education. To learn more, visit the OCR online at ed.gov/about/offices/list/ocr.

Once a 504 plan has been put into place, check in periodically with your child and your child's teachers to find out how well it is working. Let the school know if you believe there is a problem. Even when things seem to be going well, your child's 504 plan should be reviewed periodically and revised as needed. In most schools, this type of review is done yearly.

The process for obtaining a 504 plan is faster and more flexible than the IEP process, described next. A 504 plan may be a good choice for students with ADHD who are able to learn in the regular classroom with some accommodations or changes in teaching strategies. Low-intensity interventions may sometimes be included in these plans as well. On the other hand, for students who need more intensive services provided by educators with specialized training, an IEP may be a better option.

Individualized Education Program

An IEP is a blueprint for special education services—a set of instructional supports and methods that are tailored to the individual needs of students with disabilities. The process for developing and implementing an IEP is based on the *Individuals with Disabilities Education Act* (IDEA), the federal special education law.

If your teen has been identified as possibly needing special education services, an important step in the process is an evaluation to determine whether your child has a qualifying disability. This type of evaluation generally is undertaken only after other steps have been tried and proven insufficient. School personnel may refer your child for evaluation, or you may request it. In either case, you must give your consent before the evaluation can be done. To establish eligibility, two things must be shown:

- Your child falls into one of the categories of disability covered by IDEA. A category called Other Health Impairment specifically includes "attention deficit disorder or attention deficit hyperactivity disorder." Some students with ADHD may qualify under the Specific Learning Disability or Emotional/Behavioral Disability categories. ("Emotional Disturbance" is the actual term used in the law for emotional/behavioral disabilities, but that term is offensive to some.)
- The disability adversely affects your child's academic performance. For a student with ADHD, this means that

inattention, distractibility, or other ADHD-related factors have a significant and persistent impact on schoolwork.

If your child is found to be eligible for special education services, an IEP meeting is called. Meeting participants include at least one special education teacher, at least one general education teacher, other school personnel (such as a school psychologist or educational specialist), you, and sometimes your child. This group, which makes up your child's IEP team, develops a written, personalized plan for your child that states:

- How your child is currently doing in school
- What the annual academic and behavioral goals for your child are
- How progress toward these goals will be measured
- Which special education and related services will be provided
- When these services will begin, how often they will occur, and how long they will last
- How your child will be included in general education classes and school activities
- How your child will take part in standardized testing
- By age 16 (and sometimes starting younger), which transition services will be provided to help your child prepare for life after high school

You must consent to the IEP in writing before the school can start to implement it. At times, you might not see eye to eye with the school on every detail. Ideally, you and the rest of the IEP team will be able to collaborate on ironing out differences and agreeing on a plan. If you can't reach an agreement, however, disputes may be resolved through mediation or a due process hearing.

Once an IEP is in place, it's the school's job to make sure that the plan is carried out. At least once a year, the IEP should be reviewed and, if necessary, updated. However, you don't have to wait for this annual review. You or other members of the IEP team can request a revision at any time. At least every three years, your child should be re-evaluated.

An IEP can be the gateway to many helpful services. There are stringent requirements for eligibility, however. Plus, there are strict procedures for developing the IEP, putting it into action, and resolving any disputes with the school. Consequently, IEPs are often best suited for students who require a wide range of services or intensive educational support.

Educate Yourself on Navigating the System

Mastering the ins and outs of IEPs and 504 plans is no small feat. You may find yourself having to navigate a complex system and learn an unfamiliar lingo, all while trying to serve as an advocate for your child.

To make the process more manageable, every state has established at least one Parent Training and Information Center (PTI) for parents of children with disabilities. PTIs provide free information about your and your child's rights under IDEA and Section 504. They also provide guidance on other educational issues, including assessments, accommodations, dispute resolution, behavior plans, and college/work readiness. Most PTIs offer toll-free phone lines and websites, and they may host workshops, webinars, or conferences for parents as well.

Many states also have a Community Parent Resource Center (CPRC). Like PTIs, CPRCs provide free information and support to parents of children with disabilities. The difference is that CPRCs focus specifically on reaching underserved families, such as those who live in certain areas, have lower incomes, or have limited proficiency in English. Both PTIs and CPRCs are funded through IDEA.

To locate a PTI or CPRC for your state, visit parentcenterhub.org/find-your-center.

Your Role in Team Meetings

You are an important member of your teen's 504 committee or IEP team. Prepare for meetings by reviewing your teen's current 504 or IEP plan, if any, as well as recent report cards, progress reports, and notes from teachers. Write down a list of questions and concerns you want to raise at the meeting so you don't forget them.

Bone up on your and your child's legal rights, and know what to expect at the meeting. A good starting place is understood.org, a website for parents of kids with attention and learning issues that's run by a consortium of more than a dozen nonprofit groups. Consult Resources for Parents and Teens at the end of this book for more information.

At times, you may want to invite an outside professional—such as your teen's therapist or a specialist who has done an independent evaluation of your teen—to attend the meeting. (Be prepared to pay the professional for his or her time.) Or you might want to invite a parent advocate or a relative or family friend who knows your teen well. Notify the school in advance about any guests who plan to attend.

Come to the meeting ready to both share and listen. You know your child better than anyone, and you have valuable insights into your teen's interests, activities, and behavior outside of school. On the other hand, teachers see a side of your teen that you don't see, and they have expertise in educational issues. When you and the teachers put your heads together, you're more likely to fully address your teen's needs.

Classroom Accommodations for Students with ADHD

A wide variety of accommodations have been used to help students work around the effects of ADHD in the classroom. Yet, surprisingly little research has been done to determine how well these accommodations actually work. So while there is broad agreement that the right accommodations can make a difference, there isn't a lot of hard evidence to help teachers decide which changes are most likely to be effective.

Of course, teachers can draw on their experience, expertise, and knowledge of your teen to help guide the selection of accommodations. And you can improve the odds of success by sharing what works at home. But the bottom line is that finding the right accommodations for your teen may involve some trial and error.

Following are a few examples of accommodations that are often recommended for students with ADHD. Remember: There's no need to make *all* these changes. Instead, the idea is to identify ones that are effective for your teen:

- Sitting near the teacher and away from the distraction of windows
- Being provided with an extra set of textbooks to keep at home
- Breaking large projects and assignments into smaller chunks
- Receiving clear and concise directions for assignments
- Being graded only on the content of reports, not the neatness
- Having a designated quiet space for doing classwork and taking tests
- Taking short, frequent quizzes rather than one big unit test
- Receiving teacher instructions both out loud and in writing
- Being provided by the teacher with a written lesson outline
- Using a fidget object (such as a stress ball) to satisfy the need to move

What About Allowing Extra Time?

Another common accommodation for students with ADHD is allowing extra time for taking tests. In many cases, however, this change may be counterproductive. Teens with ADHD often have trouble using their time efficiently. Merely giving these teens more time to take a test just means they have more time to waste.

On the other hand, some teens with ADHD use their time well but still have trouble finishing tests as quickly as their classmates. In their case, the problem may be that they process information in their brains at a slower rate than their peers. For these teens, extending the time limit for tests could be beneficial.

The bottom line: This accommodation is probably overused, but it may be helpful for a subset of students with ADHD. Before assuming that extra time will boost your teen's test performance, ask the school to try it out and see how well it works.

Accommodations for the SAT

Students who will plan to take the SAT, PSAT/NMSQT, PSAT 10, and AP Exams can request accommodations from the College Board's Services for Students with Disabilities (collegeboard.org/students-with-disabilities). Generally speaking, going through your teen's school is the best way to make this request.

To qualify for accommodations based on ADHD, the request must

- Document your teen's diagnosis of ADHD
- Explain how participation on the exam will be impacted by ADHD
- State the accommodation being requested and why it is needed
- Show that your teen receives this accommodation when taking school tests, and present evidence demonstrating that it makes a difference in your teen's performance

As an example, some students with ADHD request extra breaks because they have trouble staying focused for long periods of time. If the request is approved, they may be given additional five-minute breaks between test sections.

A similar procedure is available for requesting accommodations on the ACT. For more information, go to act.org and search for "disabilities."

School-Based Interventions: Mentoring Programs

One challenge in middle school and high school is that your teen may not spend much time with any one teacher. Yet a teen with ADHD benefits greatly from having a support person—someone who gets to know your teen well and checks in regularly to see how things are going. To provide this kind of one-on-one connection and support, some schools have set up programs in which at-risk students are paired with school-based mentors. The mentor may be a school staff member or a trained volunteer. Two well-studied mentoring programs are Check & Connect (checkandconnect.umn.edu) and Check-In/Check-Out.

Check & Connect

Check & Connect is an intervention designed to foster greater engagement with school for students in kindergarten through 12th grade. It was originally developed by educational psychologist Sandra Christenson and her colleagues for use with disengaged students at risk of dropping out. That description certainly fits a number of students with ADHD. Two decades of research have shown that Check & Connect can increase attendance and school completion rates as well as decrease tardiness, truancy, and dropout rates.

One study included 144 ninth graders who were receiving special education services for an emotional or behavioral disability. Half were randomly assigned to take part in a Check & Connect program. Over the next four years, the Check & Connect group had better attendance and a lower dropout rate, compared to those who did not participate. The Check & Connect group also had more comprehensive college and/or career transition plans in their IEPs.

Check & Connect has four main components:

- Mentor. This is an adult with special training who works one-on-one with a student. The mentor builds a strong relationship with the student, which is focused on nurturing the student's success at school and with learning. To build this bond, the mentor commits to working with the student for at least two years. In some schools, the mentor is known as a monitor, intervention specialist, or academic coach.
- Checking. The mentor keeps an eye out for warning signs of disengagement, such as school absences, falling grades, and behavioral referrals.
- Connecting. The mentor responds to whatever is currently going on with the student. When there's a problem, the mentor works with key contacts in the school, family, and community to address it in a timely and personalized way.
- Parent involvement. The mentor also strives to build a connection between the family and the school, which helps support the student. The mentor keeps parents informed, listens to their concerns, and involves them in problem-solving.

Mentors encourage students to get actively involved in academic and school-related activities. They also try to instill a commitment to educational goals and learning. When students are engaged this way, they find school more meaningful, and they feel more invested in the future. These are key principles to keep in mind for any teen with ADHD, whether or not your school offers a formal mentoring program.

Check-In/Check-Out

Check-In/Check-Out (CICO) is another type of school-based mentoring program. It's a narrower approach, focusing on a few target behaviors rather than overall engagement. That makes it more feasible to use with a large number of students.

In CICO, the person filling the mentorship role is often called a coordinator. Typically, a student has brief, twice-a-day meetings with the same coordinator over the course of a school year. At the beginning of the day, a quick check-in meeting with the coordinator helps ensure that the student is organized for the day ahead, with all the necessary books and materials on hand and homework assignments ready to turn in.

Throughout the day, teachers evaluate the student's behavior using a daily report card. Typically, the daily report card lists two or three target behaviors that the student is working on. The card has a space for the student to make self-ratings and for each teacher to rate how well the student did on each target behavior that day. See the Sample Daily Report Card (Table 7.1) for an example of how this works.

At the end of the day, the student has a short check-out meeting with the coordinator to go over the daily report card ratings. This gives the coordinator an opportunity to reinforce areas in which the student has done well and to discuss areas in which the student has struggled. The student is also encouraged to bring the report card home and discuss it with parents. The upshot: Two important adults in the teen's life—a parent

Table 7.1
Sample Daily Report Card
Rating Scale: 0 = Never or rarely; 1 = Sometimes;
2 = Most of the time; 3 = Always

Date: October 17	Target Behavior: Completing classwork/taking notes			Target Behavior: Paying attention in class		
Class	Student rating	Teacher rating	Are both ratings the same?	Student rating	Teacher rating	Are both ratings the same?
Math	2	2	✓	2	2	✓
English	3	1		2	2	✓
Biology	2	1		3	1	
History	3	3	✓	3	2	
Spanish	2	2	✓	1	1	✓
Totals		9	3		8	3

Points Earned* (sum of the bottom row): 23

*Points can be applied toward earning a reward. A school-based mentor may work with the parent and teen to help them set appropriate goals and devise a reward system.

and a coordinator—are paying attention, and that's a powerful message in itself.

Eye to Eye

Another approach to mentoring involves having older students mentor younger ones. One example is Eye to Eye (eyetoeyenational.org), a national mentoring movement that pairs middle school students who have ADHD or learning disabilities with college and high school mentors who have those same conditions. Once a week, mentors and mentees get together as a group at a participating middle school. They work on a series of art projects that have been specifically designed for Eye to Eye. It's a fun, creative way to encourage self-expression, promote communication, and foster relationships that may have benefits for mentors and mentees alike.

More research is needed on this approach to mentoring, but it shows promise. The younger students being mentored get to know positive role models, which may help them envision bright futures for themselves. The older students serving as mentors get a self-esteem boost from being looked up to, and they may be prompted to think about their own strengths. Plus, both groups may benefit from being part of a community that accepts who they are.

Teaming Up with Your Teen's Teachers

School is a huge part of your teen's life, so it is important to know what's going on with your teen there. Getting acquainted with key school professionals—such as your teen's teachers, counselors, and mentors—helps keep you in the loop. Feedback from teachers also helps you set expectations for your teen that are high but realistic.

As kids get older, however, a dilemma often arises: Many teens don't want their parents anywhere near the school. Even if they're struggling, teens often want to deal with things on their own, and they don't want their parents involved.

To resolve this dilemma, you'll need to draw on your communication and negotiation skills. Have periodic, short discussions with your teen about how to balance your job as parent with your teen's desire for privacy. Make it clear that school is a priority, and you're committed to doing whatever you can to help your teen do well there. Talk about ways you can be involved that don't feel too intrusive or embarrassing to your teen.

Don't back down about staying involved, however. And don't try to avoid the issue by talking with school personnel behind your teen's back. If your teen finds out, the result may be distrust and resentment. Be open with your teen about any interaction you have with the school, even if the two of you aren't in complete agreement about it.

Effective Parent–Teacher Partnerships

You and your teen's teachers share a common goal: to help your teen be as successful as possible in the classroom. Here are some tips on working together effectively toward that goal:

- Have realistic expectations. If your teen is sometimes challenging to deal with at home, the same is probably true in the classroom.
- Be problem-solving partners. If one of your teen's teachers is noticing an issue in the classroom, make it clear that you would like to help address the problem. Set up a time to talk. Analyze the problem together, focusing on factors that trigger and reinforce the behavior. Then discuss ways to modify these factors. Identify what each of you will do to work with your teen on changing the behavior.
- Follow through on the plan. Do your part at home to support positive behavior at school. When the teacher puts time and energy into making the classroom changes you discussed, let the teacher know how much you appreciate it.
- Discuss how to monitor progress. Daily report cards are one way for the teacher to keep you posted on how well things are going. Grades on worksheets, quizzes, and homework may also be indicators of improvement.

Fostering Good Homework and Study Habits

Another way you can support your teen's academic progress is by encouraging good homework and study habits. That may not be easy, however. Getting homework and studying done can be a huge challenge for many teens with ADHD. Too often, parents and teens battle nightly over homework, and no one ends up feeling like the winner.

The first step toward conquering homework is knowing what the assignment is. Encourage your teen to adopt a consistent system for tracking assignments. Some teens keep everything in a three-ring binder, with papers color-coded by class. Others write down assignments in a notebook or record them using a phone app.

The next step is helping your teen learn strategies for getting homework done in a reasonable amount of time. Several years ago, Dr. Power teamed up with psychologists James Karustis and Dina Habboushe to create a program called Homework Success, which was designed to help parents of younger kids with ADHD deal with this common issue. The following tips have been adapted for adolescents:

1. Define your role. Children and younger adolescents may benefit from having a parent nearby to supervise as they do homework. By high school, however, teens often view such supervision as intrusive. At this point, you may need to take a few steps back, literally and figuratively. You and your teen can discuss and negotiate what your role in the homework process will be. It's good for your teen to know that you're there to offer guidance, support, and structure. On the other hand, it's important for you to respect your teen's growing need to work independently.

2. Break it up! Encourage your teen to break large assignments into smaller segments that can be completed in a reasonable amount of time. Have your teen write down a time limit for completing each segment (for example, 20 minutes). The Homework Chart for Teens (see Table 7.2)

Table 7.2
Homework Chart for Teens

Date: _____

Time limit: _____

What is my performance goal? (choose one)

Number of items completed: _____ (e.g., number of pages read
or sentences written)

Percentage of items correct: _____ (e.g., percentage of correctly
solved problems)

Did I reach my performance goal? (circle one)

	Points*
Yes, well above the goal	2
Yes, met the goal	1
No, below the goal	0

* Points can be applied toward earning a reward negotiated between parent and teen.

is a helpful tool for your teen to set goals and self-evalu-
ate performance.

3. Set a performance goal. Encourage your teen to write down
a performance goal for each homework segment. For math
assignments, the goal might be the percentage of problems solved correctly. For writing assignments, the goal
might be to write a paragraph with a specific number of
sentences. For reading assignments, the goal might be to
read a specific number of pages in a chapter. You can help
your teen define appropriate performance goals that are

• Measurable—The goal should be a specific action
that can be quantified.

• Reasonable—A reasonable goal is one that can be
attained by your teen about 80% of the time.

4. Get ready, get set, go! Encourage your teen to set a timer for the allotted amount of time. Then your teen can dive into doing the work.

5. Evaluate the results. When the homework segment is finished or the timer goes off, whichever comes first, your teen should stop working and assess the results. This involves your teen answering the question: *Have I achieved the performance goal set in Step 3, based on my best estimate?* If assistance is needed, you can help your teen evaluate the performance in a fair manner.

6. Celebrate success. When your teen completes all the work in the allotted time and meets or exceeds the performance goal, that's something to feel proud about. You and your teen can even establish a reward to work for (such as a trip or outing). Your teen can earn credit toward this reward by achieving homework goals.

7. Take a breather. A two- to five-minute break between homework segments gives your teen a chance to refocus.

8. Keep moving forward. Regardless of whether or not your teen met the performance goal for the last homework segment, move on to the next segment. This is very important for maintaining momentum. Your teen can always go back at the end and work on incomplete segments, if he or she has the time and energy to do so.

9. Refine the goals. After working on all the homework segments, your teen should review goals (Step 3) and results (Step 5). Your teen can then use this information to fine-tune future goals. For example, if some segments weren't completed within the time limit, your teen can think about why. Were the segments too long? If so, your teen might divide tomorrow's homework into shorter chunks.

Or was your teen distracted by something? If so, your teen might look for a quieter spot to do tomorrow's homework.

Some teens may not appreciate the support when it is offered by their parents. In these cases, it may be advisable to enlist the help of someone else—perhaps a tutor, another relative, or an older student in the neighborhood.

As you help your teen with ADHD learn strategies for setting goals and managing time, you're promoting greater success in high school. By so doing, you're equipping your teen to deal with the transition to college or a career. We'll talk about the challenges and opportunities associated with that transition in the next chapter.

Key Points

- Middle school and high school students are expected to deal with multiple teaching styles and to be well organized and self-directed. This can be challenging for students with ADHD.
- Some students with ADHD may benefit from accommodations—changes in classroom techniques or materials that are designed to level the playing field for a student with a disability. However, interventions designed mutually by teachers, students, and often parents are more likely to be successful.
- A 504 plan is commonly used to ensure that essential accommodations and services are implemented for students with ADHD.
- Students with ADHD benefit from school mentoring programs, which can help with planning, time management, and organization.
- Helping your teen learn strategies for managing homework time can promote success at school and reduce conflict at home.

Learn More

An excellent starting point for information on educational issues is the Center for Parent Information and Resources (parentcenterhub. org). For further reading about 504 plans, go to the U.S. Department of Education website (ed.gov), and search for "Section 504."

Chapter Eight

Transition to Adulthood: Supporting Independence, Staying Involved

Once your child reaches the end of high school, you might feel as if your work as a parent is nearly done. But the truth is, there's no such thing as graduating from parenthood. Your child continues to need your active involvement and emotional support, albeit in a way that reflects and respects your child's new status as a young adult.

That can be a difficult balance to achieve, but you don't have to master it overnight. Your child doesn't undergo a sudden transformation on his or her eighteenth birthday or high school graduation day. Instead, the transition to adulthood is a gradual process, and the evolution of your parent–child relationship should be gradual, too.

By this age, your child may be spending less time at home, perhaps even living elsewhere for all or much of the year. Yet it's still vital to stay connected and maintain a strong relationship. Keep the lines of communication open, and aim for back-and-forth discussions rather than one-sided lectures. Just as you did when your child was younger, look for the positive, and always be quicker to affirm than to criticize. Any 18- or

19-year-old would be lucky to have this type of relationship with a parent. But it's particularly important for a young adult who has to deal with extra challenges in daily life.

More likely than not, that description applies to your child. At least half of youth diagnosed with ADHD continue to meet the full criteria for the condition as they become adults. Even those who no longer meet the full criteria may still have some lingering symptoms. Common problems associated with ADHD in young adults include the following:

- Having difficulty paying attention, staying focused, and concentrating
- Struggling to stick with a daily schedule and make efficient use of time
- Finding it hard to be organized and get things done as intended
- Having trouble making deliberate decisions and considering consequences before acting
- Experiencing problems in college, work, or relationships that are related to ADHD symptoms

Just as at earlier ages, young adults with ADHD sometimes have coexisting conditions, which only add to the challenges they face. Common comorbidities in this age group include anxiety disorders, depression, and alcohol or drug abuse.

Making Choices About Higher Education

As high school draws to a close, you and your child must make some big decisions about what comes next. Although some might believe that going straight from high school to a four-year university is *the* pathway to success, in actuality there is no single path that's right for everyone. Many students benefit from gaining work experience or attending a community college, either prior to or instead of going the four-year college route.

If your child with ADHD has struggled with school in the past, considering a range of options may be especially beneficial. When weighing the pros and cons of different pathways, these are some factors to keep in mind:

- Four-year universities. Students attend a four-year university to earn a bachelor's degree and/or as a stepping stone to graduate school. Ultimately, a bachelor's or higher degree can open the door to a wide range of rewarding careers. Four-year universities provide unsurpassed learning opportunities that can't be found elsewhere. They also generally offer the chance to partake in an active campus life. Many students with ADHD eventually succeed in a four-year university setting, whether straight out of high school or after a few years of maturation. On the downside, this may be an expensive option. Also, at some big universities with very large classes, students who benefit from a more personal atmosphere may feel lost in the shuffle.
- Community colleges. Students attend a community college to get an associate's degree and/or earn academic credits that can later be transferred to a four-year program. Typically, community colleges are local commuter schools, which means students often live with their parents while attending classes. For some with ADHD, having a few additional years of structured family life is beneficial. Also, compared to four-year universities, community colleges may be more affordable and offer more

personalized academic attention. On the downside, it's often harder to get involved in extracurricular activities. Students usually don't live on campus, and many classmates have off-campus jobs or families of their own that keep them busy.

- Vocational or trade schools. Students attend a vocational school to obtain job training and/or certification. In general, all courses are job specific, and completing a program takes two years or less. For young adults who are turned off by school but who want a career, vocational schools may be an appealing option. Many offer extra guidance and support to help students keep up with course demands. Some programs also include internships or apprenticeships, which offer supervised entry into the world of work.

Is a Gap Year a Good Idea?

Delaying college by a year or so while gaining some real-world experience is another possible choice for recent high school graduates. Taking this route gives young people a chance to increase their maturity and gain valuable life skills before moving on to higher education. For those who found school to be a negative experience in the past, it's an opportunity to take a break from the stress and reset their expectations.

To get the most from a gap year, your child should put it to good use. That might mean practicing how to follow a regimented work schedule, gaining access to supervision on a job, and/or learning good work habits. Most paying jobs fit the bill to some extent, and they also give your child a chance to save money for college. But if paid work is hard to come by, other options include unpaid internships and volunteer positions.

On the downside, taking a gap year means getting out of the school routine for a lengthy period. That might be a concern if your child had trouble getting into school mode in the first place. You may fear that, if your child takes a break from school, he or she will never go back. One option might be for your child to take a course or two during the gap year, whether for fun or credit, to keep those academic habits intact.

Accommodations and Support Services in College

If your child chooses to pursue higher education, it's important that both of you understand what to expect. After high school, the rights of students with disabilities such as ADHD are governed by a pair of federal laws:

- *Americans with Disabilities Act* (ADA). This law prohibits discrimination against individuals with disabilities in all areas of public life, including school and work. It applies to both public and private postsecondary schools, including universities, community colleges, and vocational schools.
- Section 504 of the *Rehabilitation Act of 1973*. This law also prohibits discrimination on the basis of disability. It applies to postsecondary schools that receive federal funds, whether they are public or private institutions. (This is the same law that provides the basis for 504 plans in elementary school, middle school, and high school, but a different subsection applies to postsecondary education.)

Under these laws, a disability is defined as (1) a physical or mental impairment that substantially limits one or more major life activities, (2) having a record of such an impairment, or (3) being regarded as having such an impairment. A few examples of "major life activities" include learning, working, concentrating, and thinking.

The laws require postsecondary schools to provide equal access to both academic programs and extracurricular activities for students with qualifying disabilities. For students whose ADHD substantially limits their ability to learn and participate in the classroom, that might sometimes mean offering accommodations, such as:

- Testing in a quiet spot with reduced distractions
- Use of a digital recorder to supplement handwritten notes
- Copies of notes taken by a designated classmate
- Priority registration, so students can schedule classes at the time of day when their ADHD medication tends to be most effective

These accommodations resemble the ones used in high school. But be aware: Previous 504 plans and Individualized Education Programs (IEPs) expire upon high school graduation. To obtain accommodations in college, your child will need to apply for them once enrolled. This means informing the school that he or she has a disability and needs an academic adjustment.

Generally speaking, your child will need to provide documentation of an ADHD diagnosis by a qualified professional. Your child might also need to fill out a form specifying the requested accommodation or meet with a member of the school's disability services staff.

The college will then review your child's request. In some cases, it may agree to offer the requested accommodation. In other cases, it may work with your child to find an alternative. Keep in mind that colleges aren't required to lower or waive essential course requirements. For example, although a college might provide extended test-taking time, it wouldn't need to change the content of the test itself.

Colleges also don't have to provide services that would put an undue financial or administrative burden on the school. In addition, they aren't legally required to provide tailored or individualized services, such as tutoring or coaching.

Obtaining accommodations in college can take time, so it's wise to begin the process as early as possible. Most college websites have a page for the disability services office. Check it out during the college search process, and ask questions if anything is unclear. Ideally, if your child believes that accommodations will be necessary, he or she should be ready to submit a request as soon as the enrollment deposit is paid.

ADHD Support Services

There's a lot of variability in the disability services that colleges provide for students with ADHD. Some provide the bare minimum required by law, while others go far above and beyond to offer a supportive learning environment.

You and your child should take the quality of ADHD support services into account when choosing a college. Unfortunately, the vague descriptions of such services on websites and in brochures often aren't much help in separating the wheat from the chaff. Instead, you may need to dig a little deeper. Once you and your child have narrowed down your list to a few schools, schedule a conversation with a member of the disability services staff. If possible, arrange an in-person meeting when you tour the campus.

Here are some questions you may want to ask:

- Is there an ADHD specialist on the disability services staff?
- Does the college offer specialized academic advisement for students with ADHD?

- How complicated is the procedure for requesting accommodations?
- What kinds of accommodations are typically provided for students with ADHD?
- Are there freshmen seminars on topics such as study skills and time management?
- Is ADHD coaching available to students through the college?
- Is specialized tutoring available for students with ADHD and/or learning disabilities?
- Is there a campus support group for students with ADHD?
- Are resources available for faculty members who wish to learn more about strategies for effectively educating students with ADHD?

College Counseling Services

It's also a good idea to inquire about the college's counseling services for students. Such services are typically provided by counseling psychologists, college counselors, or social workers. The services are often provided free of charge or for a sliding-scale fee. The problems addressed may include a wide range of behavioral, emotional, interpersonal, and educational concerns. Examples include ADHD, anxiety disorders, depression, substance abuse, and eating disorders.

The transition to college is an exciting time, but it can also be stressful. College students are expected to be independent learners and deal with academic pressure. At the same time, they're trying to forge new friendships and build a personal identity. They have greater freedom to make their own choices—and sometimes their own mistakes. If they're living away from home, many also must contend with feeling homesick and missing the structure of family life.

For college students with ADHD, these issues are compounded. And in addition to ADHD, some have coexisting conditions that further complicate the adjustment to college. Many benefit from receiving counseling or therapy at some point during their college years.

Dealing with ADHD in the Workplace

By late adolescence, many young people have gotten their first taste of grown-up work, whether in a summer internship, gap year job, or college work–study program. Some have gone straight from high school into long-term employment. Whatever your child's situation, there are things he or she can do to promote greater success in the workplace.

The first step is to identify an ultimate career goal. This can help your child decide which job experiences, skills, certifications, or degrees will be needed to get from here to there. And that can help your child determine what the next step ought to be.

Certainly, the way in which ADHD affects your child as a young adult is a factor to consider when choosing a career, but it's only one piece of the puzzle. Your child's personality, interests, skills, abilities, and values should also be taken into account.

Whatever career goal your child chooses, one factor influencing success is how well ADHD and any related problems are managed. In a study of 250 adults with ADHD, the risk of long-term work difficulties was increased in those who had persistent symptoms of inattention or a greater number of coexisting conditions. This underscores the importance of maintaining healthful routines and ADHD management strategies.

A Who's Who of High-Achieving ADHDers

Having ADHD certainly does not rule out career success. In fact, a number of super-achievers from various fields have publicly discussed having ADHD. Some say they've learned to compensate for the condition, while others credit it with giving them a unique perspective on the world. Here are just a few of the individuals on the ADHD A-list:

- Adam Levine, singer
- Howie Mandel, comedian
- James Carville, political analyst
- Justin Timberlake, singer and actor
- Karina Smirnoff, dancer
- Lisa Ling, journalist
- Michael Phelps, swimmer
- Paul Orfalea, Kinko's founder
- Simone Biles, gymnast
- Terry Bradshaw, quarterback and sports commentator
- Ty Pennington, home makeover guru

Scoping Out a Dream Job

Realistically, someone brand new to the workforce may have to take whatever job comes along, at least at first. But to the extent that your child has choices, these are some characteristics to look for in an ADHD-friendly job environment:

- Clear direction and close supervision
- A supervisor who is involved and generally encouraging, rather than aloof or frequently critical
- Coworkers around the same age, with whom your child can collaborate and share mutual support
- Potential mentors—more experienced workers who aren't your child's supervisor, but who can serve as role models and advisors
- Opportunities for professional development and career advancement

Working Out Workplace Challenges

Just as in the classroom, the right strategies in the workplace can go a long way toward helping your child cope with ADHD. Following are examples of common work challenges and the types of strategies that may be helpful for managing them:

CHALLENGE: TIME MANAGEMENT

- Break large tasks into smaller subtasks.
- Create a flowchart showing the order in which subtasks should be completed.
- Set a timer to know when it's time to move on to the next subtask.
- Circle important due dates on a prominent wall or desktop calendar.

CHALLENGE: ORGANIZATION

- Use a color-coding system for papers related to different projects or activities.
- Create a "cheat sheet" to keep track of the steps in a multistep process.

CHALLENGE: INATTENTION AND DISTRACTIBILITY

- Take short, regular work breaks to restore mental focus and attention.
- Use noise-cancelling headphones to block out distracting noise.
- Minimize clutter and visual distractions in one's personal workspace.
- Request moving the workspace to a quiet spot, if feasible.

Most of these adjustments are things that your child can do on his or her own. Many bosses are also happy to assist with simple adjustments that lead to better job performance and productivity. As a rule, it's generally faster and easier to work things out this way whenever possible. For ideas on help-ful strategies, check out the U.S. Department of Labor's Job Accommodation Network at askjan.org.

Depending on the circumstances, it may also be possible for your child to request reasonable accommodations at work under the ADA. Fairly or not, the reality is that some bosses may view this as "making excuses" or "being difficult." Often, these kinds of misconceptions can be resolved through discus-sion. But if your child believes that he or she is being discrimi-nated against on the basis of a disability, it's good to know that there are legal protections in place. To learn more about your child's employment rights, visit the ADA National Network online at adata.org.

When Your Child Moves Away from Home

Whether going off to college or relocating for a job, some young adults face the prospect of moving away from home for the first time. This can be a major adjustment for the two of you, and it frequently causes some stress on both sides. To reduce the stress, try to visit the area in advance, if possible, so it doesn't feel so unfamiliar.

Talk with your child about the impending move. Listen attentively to any questions or concerns your child puts into words, and read between the lines for feelings your child may be expressing nonverbally. Be responsive to what your child communicates.

Don't be surprised if you detect some ambivalence. Although your child may be excited about the change, he or she might also be anxious about the unknown challenges ahead. In some cases, anxiety manifests as testiness or impatience. If your child reacts this way, don't take it personally. Try to be patient and consistently supportive.

To allay concerns for both of you, work with your child on planning ways to handle any challenges that might arise. Remember that people with ADHD often have trouble anticipating potential problems and planning for workable solutions. By providing support and guidance, you can be a big help to your child in this regard.

For example, let's say your child has trouble setting up and sticking with schedules. One solution might be to practice at home before the move, following a schedule similar to the one your child will have at college or work. Another solution might be to find an ADHD coach who can help your child set up a schedule, establish a reminder system, review how things are going, and look for ways to overcome obstacles.

Revisiting Medication as a Treatment for ADHD

The same types of medications used to treat ADHD in children and teens are also beneficial for young adults with the condition. However, just as at earlier ages, your child's response to a particular medication may change over time. If that happens, the doctor may adjust the amount or timing of the dose or switch to a different drug.

For a while, the doctor prescribing ADHD medication might be the same pediatrician your child has seen for years. Eventually, however, your child will probably transition to a primary care provider who treats adults—typically, a specialist in family medicine or internal medicine. To find a provider who has more than a passing familiarity with ADHD, ask your child's pediatrician for a referral. You might also want to ask around among members of your local ADHD support group.

Occasionally, the doctor managing your adult child's ADHD medication may be a neurologist or psychiatrist. Your child is more likely to see a psychiatrist if he or she is taking a medication not typically used to treat ADHD symptoms, such as an antidepressant to treat depression or anxiety.

The right ADHD medication may reduce symptoms of inattention and impulsivity. But pills alone are no substitute for skills. Your child will still need to work on setting goals, managing time, organizing activities, and self-monitoring performance. In addition, your child will need to continue practicing communication, problem-solving, and relationship building. At times, therapy may be beneficial, either alone or combined with drug treatment.

The Road from Adolescence to Adulthood

In the first chapter of this book, we promised not to sugarcoat the realities facing your child. The truth is, having ADHD makes the journey from adolescence to young adulthood more perilous and unpredictable. Rather than a smooth transition, it's often a rather bumpy ride. There may be more starts, stops, and unplanned detours.

In the long run, most adults with ADHD are able to build on their strengths and reach a good place in their lives. But there's a lot of variability, just as there is among people who don't have ADHD. In general, having adult ADHD increases the chance for greater disruption in several domains:

- Work. As a group, adults with ADHD tend to have a less consistent work history than those without the condition.

They may bounce around more from job to job or have more ups and downs in performance ratings. Ultimately, however, individuals with ADHD often have successful, fulfilling careers.

- Romantic relationships. Several studies suggest that adults with ADHD are at risk for broken relationships. Their partners also report lower levels of relationship satisfaction. But seeking treatment for ADHD and other conditions, if they arise, can be highly useful in addressing these issues.
- Parenthood. Moms and dads with ADHD may find it more difficult to be effective at parenting, especially when their children have ADHD as well. But with persistent effort—and expert guidance as needed—they can fine-tune their parenting skills.

Research shows that getting treatment for ADHD can lead to better long-term outcomes. In general, however, it doesn't completely address the effects of the condition. That's why your ongoing involvement and continued support are so crucial for your child.

You've been along for the whole ride, so you know where the potholes are. You're aware that paying attention, getting organized, managing time, and thinking before acting may come harder for your child with ADHD than for most people. But you've also seen firsthand the progress your child has made over the years. When your child falters, you can offer perspective about what worked well in the past and how far he or she has come.

Just knowing that you're there, always quick to point out what goes right and available to talk through what goes wrong, can make a huge difference. An involved, supportive parental relationship gives your child a major advantage heading into the adult years. It's a strong foundation on which to build a rewarding adult life.

Key Points

- At least half of kids diagnosed with ADHD still meet the full criteria for the condition as young adults, and many others have some lingering symptoms.
- Colleges vary widely in the ADHD support services they provide, so inquire in advance about what is available.
- Simple adjustments in the workplace can often lead to better job performance and enhanced productivity.
- A positive, supportive relationship with you continues to be important for your young adult child with ADHD.

Learn More

A good source of information and support for adults with ADHD is the Attention Deficit Disorder Association (add.org).

Glossary

accommodation   In education, a change in classroom techniques or materials that is designed to compensate for the impact of a disability on school performance.

adjunctive therapy   A treatment that is added to another treatment to boost its effects.

Affordable Care Act   A federal health care reform law, also known as Obamacare.

alpha$_2$-adrenergic agonists   A class of non-stimulant medications used to treat ADHD, including extended-release clonidine and guanfacine.

Americans with Disabilities Act   A federal civil rights law that prohibits discrimination against individuals with disabilities in all areas of public life.

amphetamine   A stimulant medication for the treatment of ADHD (brand names: Adzenys XR-ODT, Dyanavel XR, Evekeo). Some medications combine amphetamine with dextroamphetamine (brand names: Adderall, Adderall XR).

amphetamine compounds   A group of stimulant medications used to treat ADHD, including amphetamine, dextroamphetamine, and lisdexamfetamine.

antecedent   In behavioral therapy, something preceding a behavior that makes it more likely to occur.

anxiety disorders   Conditions characterized by fear or worry that is excessive, persistent, and difficult to control.

atomoxetine   A non-stimulant medication for the treatment of ADHD (brand name: Strattera).

attention-deficit/hyperactivity disorder (ADHD)   A condition characterized by persistent problems with paying attention, being overactive, and/or controlling impulsive behavior.

attention-deficit/hyperactivity disorder (ADHD) coach   A professional who helps clients with ADHD stay focused on goals, stick with plans, manage time, and prioritize activities.

authoritative parenting   A child-rearing style characterized by a high level of affection and affirmation, appropriate rule-setting, and close supervision.

behavioral contract   A written agreement between a parent and child (or teacher and student) that lays out which behaviors are being targeted for change and what the consequences of achieving or not achieving a behavioral goal will be.

behavioral therapy   A treatment that focuses on identifying behaviors to change, taking steps to make it more likely that desired behaviors will occur, and providing punishment strategically to reduce undesired behaviors.

bullying   Repeated aggressive behavior toward someone perceived as being weaker.

Children's Health Insurance Program (CHIP)   A joint federal–state program that provides health care to eligible uninsured children whose families have incomes too high for Medicaid.

clonidine, extended release   A non-stimulant medication for the treatment of ADHD (brand name: Kapvay).

Community Parent Resource Center (CPRC)   A center that provides information, guidance, and support to underserved families of children with disabilities.

comorbidity   The coexistence of two or more mental, physical, or behavioral health conditions in the same individual.

conduct disorder   A condition characterized by frequent behaviors that violate important social norms or the basic rights of others.

consequence   In behavioral therapy, something following a behavior that makes it more or less likely to occur again.

daily report cards   A strategy in which teachers evaluate students on at least one target behavior every day and send home daily reports on how the students did.

depression   A condition characterized by feeling down, empty, hopeless, or irritable for weeks on end and/or losing interest in most things that were once enjoyed.

dexmethylphenidate   A stimulant medication for the treatment of ADHD (brand names: Focalin, Focalin XR).

dextroamphetamine   A stimulant medication for the treatment of ADHD (brand names: Dexedrine Spansule, ProCentra, Zenzedi). Some medications combine amphetamine with dextroamphetamine (brand names: Adderall, Adderall XR).

disruptive mood dysregulation disorder (DMDD)   A condition characterized by persistent irritability and frequent, severe temper outbursts.

dopamine   A chemical messenger in the brain that plays a role in ADHD.

drug diversion   Selling or giving away a prescribed medication for an unlawful, non-prescribed use.

dyscalculia   A learning disorder that impairs the ability to understand and use numerical information.

dyslexia   A learning disorder that impairs the ability to read and spell.

electroencephalogram (EEG)   A test in which small, metal disks are placed on the scalp, where they pick up electrical signals from the brain and send them over attached wires to a recording device.

elimination diet   A dietary strategy that is intended to identify specific foods or food additives that may be causing symptoms in an individual.

executive function training   An intervention that uses computer-based activities involving extensive repetition and practice to strengthen specific executive functioning skills, such as working memory and behavior regulation. Also called brain training or cognitive training.

executive functioning   The brain processes involved in organizing information, planning future actions, and regulating behavior and emotions.

family therapy   A treatment approach in which at least two family members, including the child, meet jointly with a therapist to work on shared behavioral and relationship goals.

frontal lobes   Parts of each half of the brain, located behind the forehead, which are involved in cognitive activities and motor control.

gene expression   The process by which the information encoded in a gene is used to direct the production of a protein in a cell.

graduated driver licensing   A system by which young drivers gain experience behind the wheel in a gradual way designed to reduce risk.

guanfacine, extended release   A non-stimulant medication for the treatment of ADHD (brand name: Intuniv).

hyperactivity   Excessive physical movement or extreme talkativeness or restlessness.

impulsivity   Hasty actions made without giving any thought to the possible repercussions.

inattention   Difficulty staying mentally focused.

Individualized Education Program (IEP)   A blueprint for the special education services to be provided to a student with a qualifying disability under the *Individuals with Disabilities Education Act*.

Individuals with Disabilities Education Act (IDEA)   The federal special education law.

intervention   In education, a set of strategies designed through a systematic process to improve student skills, performance, or behavior.

learning disorders   Conditions that result in academic underachievement in the areas of reading, writing, and/or math skills.

lisdexamfetamine   A stimulant medication for the treatment of ADHD (brand name: Vyvanse).

Medicaid   A joint state–federal program that provides health care to individuals and families of modest means who meet eligibility requirements.

Mental Health Parity and Addiction Equity Act   A federal law that generally prevents group health plans with coverage for mental health or substance abuse services from imposing restrictions on those benefits that are less favorable than those imposed on medical and surgical benefits.

mentor   In school-based mentoring programs, a school staff member or trained volunteer who provides systematic, one-on-one support and connection to an at-risk student.

methylphenidate   A stimulant medication for the treatment of ADHD (brand names: Aptensio XR, Concerta, Daytrana, Metadate CD, Methylin Chewable Tablets, Methylin ER, Methylin Oral Solution, Quillivant XR, Ritalin, Ritalin LA, Ritalin SR).

methylphenidate compounds   A group of stimulant medications used to treat ADHD, including dexmethylphenidate and methylphenidate.

modification   In education, an adjustment in lesson content or learning expectations for a student with a disability.

Multimodal Treatment of ADHD   A major study that examined the long-term effectiveness of medication, behavioral therapy, or both.

negative reinforcement   The removal of something unpleasant following a behavior, making it more likely that the behavior will be repeated.

neurofeedback   An intervention that measures electrical activity inside a person's brain associated with focused attention and provides real-time feedback to improve attention and concentration.

neuropsychological tests   Standardized tasks to evaluate psychological processes that are related to particular brain structures and functions.

norepinephrine   A chemical messenger in the brain that is thought to play a role in ADHD.

norepinephrine reuptake inhibitor   A class of non-stimulant medication used to treat ADHD, including atomoxetine.

oppositional defiant disorder (ODD)   A condition characterized by an ongoing pattern of frequent defiance, hostility, and spitefulness.

organizational skills training   A behavioral intervention that focuses on helping students learn to organize school materials, keep track of homework assignments, and manage homework and study time.

parent training   A treatment approach in which parents work with a therapist to improve their communication, relationship building, and behavior management skills.

Parent Training and Information Center (PTI)   A center that provides information, guidance, and support to parents of children with disabilities.

planned ignoring   The intentional withholding of attention as a method of reducing annoying but harmless behaviors.

positive reinforcement   Something pleasant or rewarding that follows a behavior, making it more likely that the behavior will be repeated.

prefrontal cortex   A region of the brain, composed of the front part of the frontal lobes, which plays a key role in organization, planning, and self-control.

prescription assistance program   A program, run by the state or a pharmaceutical company, which provides free or low-cost medications to qualifying individuals.

punishment   Something unpleasant or aversive that follows a behavior, making it less likely that the behavior will be repeated.

Section 504 of the Rehabilitation Act of 1973   A federal civil rights law that prohibits discrimination on the basis of disability.

Section 504 plan   An educational plan that outlines accommodations and services to be implemented for a student with a disability.

special education services   A set of instructional supports and methods that are tailored to the individual needs of students with disabilities.

stimulants   The best studied and most widely prescribed class of medications for ADHD, including amphetamine compounds and methylphenidate compounds.

strategic punishment   The deliberate, judicious use of punishment as a method of deterring serious rule infractions or harmful behavior.

tics   Sudden, rapid, repetitive movements or vocalizations over which one has little or no control.

Tourette syndrome   A disorder in which movement and vocal tics generally occur many times throughout the day.

working memory   A limited-capacity brain system for temporarily holding and manipulating information.

Resources for Parents and Teens

Organizations

- Attention Deficit Disorder Association (ADDA), add.org, (800) 939-1019. A membership organization providing information and networking opportunities for adults with ADHD, including college students.
- Children and Adults with Attention-Deficit/Hyperactivity Disorder (CHADD), chadd.org, (800) 233-4050. A membership organization providing education, advocacy, and support for individuals of all ages with ADHD and their families.

Websites

- ADDitude, additudemag.com
- American Academy of Child and Adolescent Psychiatry, aacap.org
- American Academy of Pediatrics, healthychildren.org
- American Psychological Association, apa.org
- Association for Behavioral and Cognitive Therapies, abct.org
- Child Mind Institute, childmind.org
- Eye to Eye, eyetoeyenational.org
- National Institute of Mental Health, nimh.nih.gov
- Society of Clinical Child and Adolescent Psychology, effectivechildtherapy.org
- Understood (National Center for Learning Disabilities), understood.org

Books

- Barkley, Russell A. *Taking Charge of ADHD: The Complete, Authoritative Guide for Parents*. 3rd ed. New York: Guilford Press, 2013.
- Barkley, Russell A., and Arthur L. Robin. *Your Defiant Teen: 10 Steps to Resolve Conflict and Rebuild Your Relationship*. 2nd ed. New York: Guilford Press, 2014.
- Gold, Jodi. *Screen-Smart Parenting: How to Find Balance and Benefit in Your Child's Use of Social Media, Apps and Digital Devices*. New York: Guilford Press, 2014.
- Grossberg, Blythe. *Applying to College for Students with ADD or LD: A Guide to Keep You (and Your Parents) Sane, Satisfied and Organized Throughout the Admission Process*. Washington, DC: Magination Press, 2011.
- Hallowell, Edward M., and John J. Ratey. *Driven to Distraction: Recognizing and Coping with Attention Deficit Disorder from Childhood Through Adulthood*. New York: Anchor Books, 2011.
- Langberg, Joshua M. *Improving Children's Homework, Organization and Planning Skills (HOPS): A Parent's Guide*. Bethesda, MD: National Association of School Psychologists, 2014.
- Maitland, Theresa E. Laurie, and Patricia O. Quinn. *Ready for Take-Off: Preparing Your Teen with ADHD or LD for College*. Washington, DC: Magination Press, 2011.
- Nadeau, Kathleen. *The ADHD Guide to Career Success: Harness Your Strengths, Manage Your Challenges*. New York: Routledge, 2016.
- Nadeau, Kathleen G., Ellen B. Littman, and Patricia O. Quinn. *Understanding Girls with ADHD: How They Feel and Why They Do What They Do*. Washington, DC: Advantage Books, 2016.
- Quinn, Patricia O. *AD/HD and the College Student: The Everything Guide to Your Most Urgent Questions*. Washington, DC: Magination Press, 2012.
- Quinn, Patricia O., and Theresa E. Laurie Maitland. *On Your Own: A College Readiness Guide for Teens with ADHD/LD*. Washington, DC: Magination Press, 2011.
- Spodak, R., and K. Stefano. *Take Control of ADHD: The Ultimate Guide for Teens with ADHD*. Waco, TX: Prufrock Press, 2011.
- Wilens, Timothy E., and Paul G. Hammerness. *Straight Talk About Psychiatric Medications for Kids*. 4th ed. New York: Guilford Press, 2016.

Resources for Coexisting Conditions

Anxiety and Depression
- Anxiety and Depression Association of America, adaa.org
- Depression and Bipolar Support Alliance, dbsalliance.org

Learning Disorders
- LD OnLine, ldonline.org
- Learning Disabilities Association of America, ldaamerica.org
- National Center for Learning Disabilities, ncld.org

Substance Abuse (Alcohol, Drugs, and Tobacco)
- National Institute on Alcohol Abuse and Alcoholism, niaaa.nih.gov
- National Institute on Drug Abuse, drugabuse.gov
- National Institute on Drug Abuse for Teens, teens.drugabuse.gov
- Partnership for Drug-Free Kids, drugfree.org
- Smokefree Teen (National Cancer Institute), teen.smokefree.gov
- Stop Underage Drinking (Interagency Coordinating Committee on the Prevention of Underage Drinking), stopalcoholabuse.gov
- The Cool Spot (National Institute on Alcohol Abuse and Alcoholism), thecoolspot.gov
- Too Smart to Start (Substance Abuse and Mental Health Services Administration), toosmarttostart.samhsa.gov

Tourette Syndrome
- Tourette Association of America, tourette.org

Resources for School Issues

- Center for Parent Information and Resources, parentcenterhub.org
- U.S. Department of Education, ed.gov
- U.S. Department of Education: Individuals with Disabilities Education Act, idea.ed.gov

Resources for Work Issues

- ADA National Network, adata.org
- Job Accommodation Network, askjan.org

Books for ADHD Professionals

- American Psychiatric Association. *Diagnostic and Statistical Manual of Mental Disorders.* 5th ed. Washington, DC: American Psychiatric Publishing, 2013.
- Barkley, Russell A., ed. *Attention-Deficit Hyperactivity Disorder: A Handbook for Diagnosis and Treatment.* 4th ed. New York: Guilford Press, 2014.
- Barkley, Russell A., and Arthur L. Robin. *Defiant Teens: A Clinician's Manual for Assessment and Family Intervention.* 2nd ed. New York: Guilford Press, 2014.
- Daly, Brian P., Aimee K. Hildenbrand, and Donald T. Brown. *ADHD in Children and Adolescents.* Boston: Hogrefe, 2016.
- Evans, Steven W., and Betsy Hoza, eds. *Treating Attention Deficit Hyperactivity Disorder: Assessment and Intervention in Developmental Context.* Kingston, NJ: Civic Research Institute, 2011.
- Gregg, Noël. *Adolescents and Adults with Learning Disabilities and ADHD: Assessment and Accommodation.* New York: Guilford Press, 2009.
- Langberg, Joshua M. *Homework, Organization and Planning Skills (HOPS) Interventions: A Treatment Manual.* Bethesda, MD: National Association of School Psychologists, 2011.
- Power, Thomas J., James L. Karustis, and Dina F. Habboushe. *Homework Success for Children with ADHD: A Family-School Intervention Program.* New York: Guilford Press, 2001.
- Scales, Peter C., and Nancy Leffert. *Developmental Assets: A Synthesis of the Scientific Research on Adolescent Development.* Minneapolis, MN: Search Institute, 2004.
- Schultz, Brandon K., and Steven W. Evans. *A Practical Guide to Implementing School-Based Interventions for Adolescents with ADHD.* New York: Springer, 2015.
- Sibley, Margaret H. *Parent-Teen Therapy for Executive Function Deficits and ADHD Building Skills and Motivation.* New York: Guilford Press, 2016.

Index

References to tables and boxes are denoted by an italicized *t* and *b*.